MEMORIZE
THIS

TH1NK
™

Go   Ahead:

TH1NK: *about God*

about life

about others

Faith isn't just an act; it's something you live—something huge and sometimes unimaginable. By getting into the real issues in your life, TH1NK books open opportunities to talk honestly about your faith, your relationship with God and others, as well as all the things life throws at you.

Don't let other people th1nk for you . . .

TH1NK for yourself.

www.th1nkbooks.com

MEMORIZE THIS

TMS 3.0

by d. mason rutledge

TH1NK Books
an imprint of NavPress®

NavPress
P.O. Box 35001
Colorado Springs, Colorado 80935

The Navigators is an international Christian organization. Our mission is to reach, disciple, and equip people to know Christ and to make Him known through successive generations. We envision multitudes of diverse people in the United States and every other nation who have a passionate love for Christ, live a lifestyle of sharing Christ's love, and multiply spiritual laborers among those without Christ.

NavPress is the publishing ministry of The Navigators. NavPress publications help believers learn biblical truth and apply what they learn to their lives and ministries. Our mission is to stimulate spiritual formation among our readers.

ISBN 1-57683-457-3

Cover and interior design by BURNKIT (www.burnkit.com)
Creative Team: Jay Howver, Eric Stanford, Kathy Mosier, Pat Miller

Some of the anecdotal illustrations in this book are true to life and are included with the permission of the persons involved. All other illustrations are composites of real situations, and any resemblance to people living or dead is coincidental.

Printed in Canada

1 2 3 4 5 6 7 8 9 10 / 07 06 05 04 03

FOR A FREE CATALOG OF
NAVPRESS BOOKS & BIBLE STUDIES,
CALL 1-800-366-7788 (USA)
OR 1-416-499-4615 (CANADA)

*"To the people of my hometown church,
Maple Park Lutheran Brethren,
who taught me the importance of Scripture."*

CONTENTS

INTRODUCTION

Life is a journey. It is full of excitement, adventure, and fun.

The most significant event in this journey happened when you met Christ and made Him your Savior. That event may have felt like the end of your journey, and in a sense it was, but it was also the beginning. Your old journey ended and a new journey began (see 2 Corinthians 5:17).

When you committed your life to Christ, you were most likely promised a new life of excitement, adventure, and fun. And certainly that's what the Christian life can be. There is nothing that compares to walking through life with Jesus. In fact, He came to give you life to the full (see John 10:10).

What you may not have realized at the time, though, is that this new life with Christ would also have its challenges, struggles, and difficulties. Have you discovered that yet?

Memorize This is designed to assist you in each stage of this new journey. It will help you celebrate the excitement, adventure, and fun, as well as carry you through the challenges, struggles, and difficulties of life.

But *Memorize This* is only an aid. It will introduce you to another book, the Bible, in which you can find divine wisdom for living. Think of God's Word as a map for your life journey.

MAP FOR THE JOURNEY

My children have a map they enjoy looking at called *The Big, Big, Big World Atlas*. Its two-by-three-foot cardboard pages have large, colorful maps of the world's continents. The maps not only include titles and borders but also contain descriptive pictures. For example, there are pictures of the Space Needle in Seattle, mountains in Colorado, and wooden shoes in Holland. While these maps are colorful and somewhat informative, they are not maps we use to navigate our family trips.

When we want to get somewhere, there is another map we use, which we keep in the car. This compact, folded map is not so colorful, but it is very informative. When we are unsure of the route to a place, it helps us find the way. If we make a wrong turn, it redirects us. During the course of our trip, it confirms that we are going in the right direction.

In the same way, the Bible serves as a map for our journey through life with Christ. It is one of the key tools God has given us.

Many people want to receive directions like those given by *The Big, Big, Big World Atlas*. They might say, "Give me the big, colorful pictures and a general sense of my place in the world, but don't get specific with the direction of my life."

The Psalms, however, say that God's Word is a light unto our path (see Psalm 119:105). We are to use a map that will give us details. Unlike *The Big, Big, Big World Atlas*, the Bible gives specific direction. It may not be as colorful, but it is packed with information that will help you get where you are going. As you become more familiar with the information in the Bible, the person it speaks of—Jesus Christ—will become more real in your life.

THE JOURNEY IN STAGES

Just as a journey changes as you move forward, so does your walk with Christ. One of the greatest challenges for you as a follower of Christ is to overcome the belief that you have finally arrived. There is no "arriving" until the "eternal arrival."

Nevertheless, it is common for followers of Christ to plateau. They attain a certain level of knowledge where they feel comfortable and then do not pursue further growth. This is dangerous in any endeavor. For example, in learning to snowboard, you don't stay on the green runs (beginner level) forever. Having attained competency in green runs, you move forward to the blue runs (intermediate level). To stay on the green runs would be boring. It wouldn't be all that snowboarding can be.

> *Leaders who plateau early reveal a common pattern. They learn new skills until they can operate comfortably within them, but then fail to seek new skills deliberately and habitually. They coast on prior experience.*[1]
>
> —J. ROBERT CLINTON

This is something to be careful of in your journey with Christ as well. The Bible says that as we mature in our faith, we should be like people who grow up from babyhood and progress from drinking milk to eating meat (see Hebrews 5:12-14). Spiritually speaking, some are not ready for meat and must continue with milk because they are immature. This is not healthy. Your walk with Christ must move forward for you to experience all that Christ has planned for your life.

Memorize This is a tool primarily for high school and first- and second-year college students. It is a progressive building tool in four stages. Each stage is designed to encourage your growth in Christ. Don't rush it. In fact, I recommend that you take a year for each stage, perhaps even two years for the second and third stages. Use each stage as you are ready for it in your life journey.

When you complete a stage of this journey, make sure you celebrate. (You may even want to celebrate after each individual topic.) To complete a stage is a great accomplishment, and you deserve dinner out—super-sized.

Now let's look more closely at the four stages around which *Memorize This* is organized:

Stage One: New Believer. The first phase is intended for those who have just met Christ or for those who are beginning their own faith journey. For example, it would be perfect for someone who has recently completed confirmation. The focus is on assurance—assurance of God's love, of who Jesus is, of your salvation, and so on.

Stage Two: Growing Disciple. The second phase is meant for those who are in a discipling relationship. Each phase is best completed (whether individually or as part of a group) under the direction of a mature believer, but this is especially true with the second phase. Do yourself a favor and complete this phase under the direction of a mature Christian who will make himself or herself available for discussion on the topics.

Stage Three: Life Issues. This phase is designed for high school seniors or college freshmen. It examines the challenges of an adult journey with Christ, including humility, purity, prayer, and so forth.

Stage Four: Leadership. This final stage builds upon the three previous stages and provides verses for young people in Christian leadership. These verses primarily focus on how we can show our faith.

USING THIS TOOL

As a progressive guide to your life journey with Christ, *Memorize This* serves several purposes. Use it as a discipleship tool, a Bible study, and a Scripture memory system.

Discipleship. As I have already said, I recommend that you work on *Memorize This* with another person or group. It can be a friend or small group of friends with whom you commit to working on the verses and studies. It can also be a mentor, an older, more experienced follower of Christ who will walk with you through the stages.

Your *Memorize This* partner needs to be committed to you, to the Bible, and to the process. This is important. Your partner must be willing to meet with you and quiz you on the verses. He or she must be willing to study the Bible with you. Finally, this partner must be committed to the details and to the excellence that successful completion of this program requires.

Bible study. As you work through *Memorize This*, you will dig into many key portions of God's Word. So as you're memorizing verses, you'll also be learning more of the meaning of the special book God has given us for our good.

To maximize the Bible study function of the program, focus on more than just the memory verses. Open your Bible and read the chapter in which the verse is located as well as the chapters before and after. Do not allow these verses to live in isolation. Draw them from the context of the narrative. You'll learn so much more that way.

Scripture memory. Of course, the primary use of *Memorize This* is as a tool to help you memorize passages of the Bible. The Bible says that if we focus on the Word of God, we will not sin against God (see

Psalm 119:11). Memorization helps us focus on Scripture like nothing else.

One tool for memorizing Scripture that has proved successful for decades is the *Topical Memory System (TMS)* developed by The Navigators. *Memorize This* is an updated version of the *Topical Memory System;* that's why it is subtitled *TMS* 3.0. It has been carefully adapted for today's teenage and college-age followers of Christ. It works.

Have you ever focused your energy on accomplishing a task? Maybe it was to play a varsity sport. Maybe it was to get Mario through the castle. Maybe it was to get a good grade in a class. Whatever the task, your effort paid off.

Bible verse memorization will pay off big-time for you. It will change your personal relationships, improve your walk with Jesus, and give you a new outlook on life.

It is critical, therefore, that you are disciplined in this effort. To reap the long-term benefits of verse memorization, you must be consistent and well organized in this work.

Yet if you do fall behind, don't give up. Pick up where you left off and go for it! There will be periods when you are simply too busy to invest as much time as you would like to; that's natural. So be disciplined, but give yourself grace. Just never quit.

> *If you slip and stumble and forget God for an hour, and assert your old proud self, and rely upon your own clever wisdom, don't spend too much time in anguished regrets and self-accusations but begin again, just where you are.*[2]
>
> —THOMAS KELLY

At the same time, it is important to be exact. Be word-perfect. If you miss a word or say a wrong word in repeating a verse, go back and start over immediately. Make sure that whoever is checking verses for you knows that the standard is perfection.

Memorize not only the verse itself but also the topic title and verse reference. To have a number of unorganized verses floating in our minds is not as helpful as having the structure provided by this program.

When memorizing a verse, start with the topic—for example, "Assurance of Eternal Life." Then say the reference, such as "John 3:16." Follow that by an exact reciting of the verse. End by repeating the reference: "John 3:16." It is important that you carefully follow this pattern to memorize your verses because it has been proven to work best.

In summary, *Memorize This* is three tools in one: a discipleship tool, a Bible study, and a Scripture memory system. Use it for all it's worth.

YOU CAN MAKE THE JOURNEY

You have so much work to do. Your time is divided among school, work, friends, sports, church, homework, and on, and on. It's difficult to commit to a new program, especially something that involves memorization. You already have to memorize a lot for school.

Yet *Memorize This* is one effort that will impact every part of your life. It will be difficult at first, but as you continue, you will see changes in your attitude, your relationships, and your journey with Christ. These changes will encourage you all the more.

You can do it! God will be with you in this effort. In addition, your mentor, partner, or group will motivate you to keep going.

Carry your verses with you, and when you have downtime, go through them. Waiting at stoplights, go through your verses. Standing in line for your grande white chocolate mocha, go through your verses. Riding the bus to the away game, go through your verses. Work on your verses all the time.

Each verse is included in four Bible versions on cards in the back of this book. Choose the translation of each verse that you like best and memorize that one. Organize or re-create the verses in a manner that works best for you. You may want to have them laminated on sheets. You may want to burn them as an audio file on CD and listen to them. You may want to put them on a handheld device. Do what you need to do.

Also, find the best time and place for you to do your memorization work. Some find it best to review the verses first thing in the morning or before they go to sleep at night. Others do it during lunch or at a coffee shop. And still others work on them during a walk around the neighborhood or on a hike. Whenever and wherever you do it, make sure you have a consistent schedule to work on your verses. Your small group or mentor can help you with this system.

You are starting on a magnificent journey. At times it will be difficult. This will be true especially in the beginning as your mind and soul are stretched in a new direction. Realize that you are training for a marathon, not a sprint.

There will also be amazing times as you memorize these verses and work through the study. You will sense God bringing verses to your mind to bless you and others. You will see that the benefits are completely worth the effort.

Have a great time and enjoy the journey! Now memorize this . . .

NEW BELIEVER

We begin the *Memorize This* endeavor by breaking down the eight core components of assurance that every follower of Christ ought to have. They include:

- Assurance of God's love for you and the world
- Assurance of who Jesus is
- Assurance of your own forgiveness
- Assurance of strength for this journey
- Assurance of an answer to prayer
- Assurance of your salvation
- Assurance of guidance during the journey

Your faith journey with Jesus is something you need to be sure of. You need to know that God loves you. You need to understand that Jesus actually walked this earth. You need to believe that you are forgiven.

Your faith journey certainly didn't start with assurances. It most likely started with a number of questions—questions that probably still bounce around in your head like lotto balls trying to come up with the winning combination. But there's no reason why you can't proceed with assurance. And that means having faith.

Faith is not intelligent understanding, faith is deliberate commitment to a Person where I see no way. [1]

—OSWALD CHAMBERS

You will rarely have enough assurance of God's love, your own forgiveness, or any of the other topics listed earlier. Your journey with Jesus is going to depend a great deal on your faith in Him and what He has done. This is the ground you want to build upon.

Jesus once told the story of two house builders. (You've probably heard the story and sung the song. Do you remember?) One built his house on sand and the other built his house on a rock. When the storm came, the house built on the rock remained standing and provided its owner with shelter, but the man who built his house upon the sand lost everything (see Matthew 7:24-27).

Now that your journey has begun, it's time to grow in your assurance. The answers may never be 100 percent, but you can grow in your assurance of the answers.

Memorize this and grow not only in your assurance but also in your faith.

CHAPTER ONE

ASSURANCE OF GOD'S LOVE

God absolutely loves you. Do you know that? It's hard to get our mind around, but it is true. He loves you.

> *Becoming the Beloved means letting the truth of our Belovedness become enfleshed in everything we think, say and do.*[1]
>
> —HENRI J. M. NOUWEN

This is where the faith journey starts: understanding that God loves you. If you do not have an assurance of God's love, your faith journey will not last long.

Memorize this and you will grow in your assurance of God's love:

- Psalm 86:5
- Zephaniah 3:17
- Romans 5:5
- 1 Kings 8:23

5/16/05

THE GOOD GOD

You are forgiving and good, O Lord,
     abounding in love to all who call to you. (Psalm 86:5)

It is not advisable to experience the verses in *Memorize This* in isolation. That can be a dangerous practice. Each verse shared is part of a larger book and the total of God's love letter to us—the Bible.

In that light, read all of Psalm 86. Then jot down things that stand out to you in the psalm.

you alone are God
great is your love toward me
compassionate & gracious God
abounding in love & faithfulness
comfort

Psalms is unlike most other books in the Bible. It could be called a songbook or book of poetry because the psalms were used by believers to worship the Lord.

Did you notice how small capital letters were used in several places to refer to God in the psalm? When you see "LORD" in the Bible, that reads *YHWH* in the original Hebrew text. You may have heard it pronounced *Yahweh*. It is the most reverent and holy name used for God in the Bible.

Yahweh was considered to be a mysterious God. The Israelites respected and even feared Him. After all, this was the God who destroyed whole cities. His followers approached Him with caution.

David, the writer of Psalm 86, was king of Israel and one of the most incredible individuals of history. God said David was a man after God's own heart. But David was also a man who had some struggles along his life journey. He had an affair and was a murderer. He was a sinner just like you and me.

Read Psalm 86 again. How does your new insight into God and the author of this psalm change your perspective on it? Jot down some thoughts.

Although God is mysterious, David believes he (God) will save, deliver, comfort, and above all love David. How? David doesn't know, but he has faith.

God is still mysterious. We don't know why certain things happen in our lives. And we are still sinners. We do things that we know God would rather we not do.

With this in mind, write your own personal paraphrase of Psalm 86:5.

You see past our sin to your image in us, Lord, and you will provide abundant love to those who look to you.

THE GOD WHO IS WITH US

5/18/05

"The LORD your God is with you,
   he is mighty to save.
He will take great delight in you,
   he will quiet you with his love,
   he will rejoice over you with singing."
(Zephaniah 3:17)

For context, read Zephaniah 3. Zephaniah was a prophet. A prophet is one who speaks the words of God. Let's break this verse down.

"The LORD your God is with you." What does this mean? When have you experienced God with you?

You are never alone, God is always there.

"He is mighty to save." This is a powerful, life-changing line. Our God is not a wimp. He is able and ready to save us from anything. He is in charge.

Sometimes it is hard to see how God has saved us. He may be saving us all the time and we don't see it.

The movie *Signs* gives us a great picture of how God saves us. In the movie, the world is under attack by space aliens who come to the home of Graham, a former Episcopal priest, played by Mel Gibson. Graham's son has asthma, and during the attack, the son nears death because of his condition. Graham hates God because God has given his son this condition, and his son is unable to breathe. But when an alien tries to kill Graham's son with poison, the poison does not enter his body because the asthma has closed his lungs. Graham realizes that the asthma has actually saved his son's life. Earlier in the story, the last words of Graham's dying wife to her husband were "Graham . . . see!"

Do you "see"? God is saving you all the time. How can you enhance your ability to see God working in your life? It begins by asking, "God, help me to see." It continues by looking for His action in your life. It concludes by writing it down.

God will move in your life this week. Jot a few lines about the experience. See!

It seems every day ends with a miracle here. And whatever God may be, I thank God for this day.

—LIEUTENANT DUNBAR IN *DANCES WITH WOLVES*

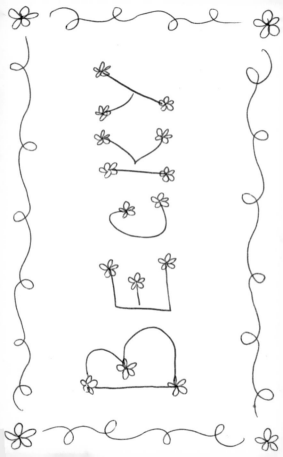

"He will take great delight in you." God not only loves you; He likes you. Sometimes love can feel like a requirement: *I have to love my sister, because we're in the same family.* It's way more than this for God. He really likes to hang out with you, like a best friend.

"He will quiet you with his love." Often we are quieted with a shout—*Hey, shut up!* Zephaniah said that God will quiet us with His love. Have you ever been quieted by love? It's like melting.

Finally, "He will rejoice over you with singing." You make God sing!

Draw a picture of this verse. It doesn't have to be a great painting, just a simple picture of what it means for you to experience God as expressed by Zephaniah in the verse.

GOD OF LOVE

Hope does not disappoint us, because God has poured out his love into our hearts by the Holy Spirit, whom he has given us. (Romans 5:5)

Read Romans 5. The book of Romans is in the New Testament. We experience God at a new level in the New Testament, as compared to the Old Testament.

How can you see this new relationship with God expressed in this verse?

Many Bible versions title sections within the chapter. What title does your Bible version give for this section?

This verse talks about three feelings: hope, disappointment, and love. How have you experienced these three?

- Hope:

- Disappointment:

- Love:

Write about a personal relationship that has included all three.

How is your relationship with God similar to this relationship?

God has called you into a special love relationship, one based on hope. These assurances are building on that hope. But there will be disappointments. There will be times when you disappoint God and times when you are disappointed by Him. It is for those times that He has provided the Holy Spirit to pour love into your being.

The deepest of relationships experience times of hope, disappointment, and love. These times deepen our love even more.

THE GOD OVER ALL

O Lord, God of Israel, there is no God like you in heaven above or on earth below—you who keep your covenant of love with your servants who continue wholeheartedly in your way. (1 Kings 8:23)

This passage does not live in isolation; it is part of a larger story. It's a long chapter, but read all of 1 Kings 8 for context. What is the larger story in this passage?

Prayer is an important part of our relationship with God. It is one of the primary ways we communicate with Him. This prayer demonstrates that.

Verse 23 talks about gods in heaven and on the earth. At the time it was written, many people worshiped idols. For the most part, we do not have statue idols today, though we may still have things in our lives that we treat like idols.

God in heaven we can understand, but what are gods on earth? What idols do people worship here on earth?

A covenant is a contract. We have a contract of love with God if we wholeheartedly pursue Him. What does it mean for you to wholeheartedly pursue God?

Write a covenant of love with God, and include the aspects found in this prayer. Name the "earthly gods" in your life, express how you will continue to wholeheartedly follow the one true God, and so on.

CHAPTER TWO

ASSURANCE OF JESUS

Jesus is the most incredible person to ever have walked this earth. There are very few people—agnostic, atheistic, or otherwise—who would argue against that fact. They may have other issues with Christ and Christianity, but they would not deny that Jesus was a great teacher and a great man. One example of His influence in our world is that our calendar is based upon Jesus' life; we number the year according to the time that has passed since He walked with us.

Jesus is amazing for many reasons. He was an unbelievable motivator. Working with a team of twelve and a ministry area that would barely cover one of the smallest U.S. states, He changed the way the world operates. He was also a remarkable leader. Most of our greatest world leaders headed armies. Jesus had no army; in fact, His way was love and peace. Finally, He was a miracle worker. Jesus performed individual and group miracles, and many believe He continues to do miracles today.

The most amazing thing is that Jesus claimed to be "God in a bod." The God who created the universe came to earth as one of us. As Eugene Peterson says in *The Message*, Jesus moved into our neighborhood (see John 1:14).

Jesus is the basis of everything we have from God and in God today. Memorize this and you will have greater assurance of Jesus:

- John 14:6
- Matthew 1:21

- Luke 24:39-40
- Hebrews 1:3

THE WAY

Jesus answered, "I am the way and the truth and the life. No one comes to the Father except through me." (John 14:6)

For context, read chapters 13 and 14 in the gospel of John.

John 14:6 is one of Jesus' most exclusive and incredible claims. Jesus was saying, "There is only one way to God, and it is me." That's bold. In a world where we are told there are many spiritual options, God provides only one way to know Him: Jesus. There is no other way.

How does this strike you? Be honest.

Who did Jesus tell this to?

Where was Jesus when He said these words? (You may have to look back a chapter or two in the Bible to find the answer.)

Why do you think Jesus was saying this to these people at this time?

Have you ever been in a tough situation and felt better when somebody took control? It gives you comfort when someone stands up and says, "Follow me," doesn't it? This was Jesus' claim in this passage.

Remember Jack and Rose in the movie *Titanic*? When the ship started to go down, Jack began to shout commands. Rose didn't question or second-guess Jack; she accepted his directives. This was no time for her to say, "Wait, Jack, let's consider the numerous options to save ourselves." She followed and lived.

Now Jesus is neither Jack nor a crisis intervention counselor; He is God. His claim is not just one of control or comfort, but one of certainty. This is *the* way.

Ours is one of the most difficult times in which to live. The world is quickly changing. For many it feels like the chaos of a sinking ship. Jesus stands in the midst of that chaos and makes a bold claim: "Follow me."

Read John 14:6 again. Reflect upon what Jesus said in light of the chaotic world in which you live. Now how does His bold claim make you feel?

As you continue on a journey full of ups and downs, may you find comfort in Jesus, a man who is strong enough and sure enough to make the boldest statement ever made.

SAVIOR SENT FROM ABOVE

She will give birth to a son, and you are to give him the name Jesus, because he will save his people from their sins. (Matthew 1:21)

Read Matthew 1:18-25.

Who is speaking in Matthew 1:21?

To whom is he speaking?

Explain the situation surrounding Matthew 1:21 that led to this dream.

Place yourself in that situation. What would you expect to hear from God?

We have already expressed the incredible nature of Jesus. Can you imagine such an amazing Person coming into the world amid such controversy? Write down the headlines that newspapers might have used if they were reporting on this event.

It was under these circumstances that our Savior entered the world.

REALLY RESURRECTED

> "Look at my hands and my feet. It is I myself! Touch me
> and see; a ghost does not have flesh and bones, as you see
> I have."
>
> When he had said this, he showed them his hands
> and feet. (Luke 24:39-40)

What title does your Bible give to the section that includes this
passage? What would you title this passage?

To gain context for these verses, read Luke 24.

Who was Jesus talking to in Luke 24:39-40?

Look at Luke 22. What happened to the disciples in this chapter?

Look at Luke 23. What happened to Jesus in this chapter?

With that context, put yourself in the room with the disciples.
Get a picture in your mind of what the room looks like — the
floor, walls, ceiling, doors, and windows. Imagine the conversation
going on among those in the room prior to Jesus' entering. Now

write a dialogue between yourself and Jesus that might follow Luke 24:39-40.

DIVINE SON

> The Son is the radiance of God's glory and the exact representation of his being, sustaining all things by his powerful word. After he had provided purification for sins, he sat down at the right hand of the Majesty in heaven. (Hebrews 1:3)

For a more complete picture of the Divine Son, read all of Hebrews 1.

Hebrews 1:3 describes who Jesus is, what He did, and what He does today. The first sentence gives three facts about Jesus. Identify these three and explain each.

1.

2.

3.

How did Jesus provide purification for sins? Look up 1 Peter 3:18 for assistance.

Some extraordinary things are said about Jesus in Hebrews 1:3 and 1 Peter 3:18. Remember that while Jesus was all this, He was also human. Look up the following three verses from the gospel of John and explain how they show Jesus' humanness:[1]

- John 4:6:

- John 4:7:

- John 11:35:

Finally, Jesus now sits next to God as our friend, advocate, and intermediary. When Jesus and God talk about you, what do they say? Write out what you think it might be.

Jesus was and still is amazing in His personhood, in His saving action, and in His continuing work with God. Any one of these qualities alone would be incredible. That one Man would encompass all three is miraculous.

CHAPTER THREE

ASSURANCE OF FORGIVENESS

While we can read the verses and believe what they say, it is still difficult at times to completely comprehend the fact that we are actually forgiven. This fact is hard to grasp because we know how bad we have been. Old sins and things we have done in the past can nag at us. They can tear at our confidence and our ability to believe that we are actually forgiven. They can make us feel less than adequate, unworthy of all that God has done for us.

Memorize this and you will have greater assurance of the forgiveness of your sins:

- Acts 10:43
- Isaiah 53:5
- 1 Peter 2:24
- Ephesians 1:7-8

SOURCE OF FORGIVENESS

All the prophets testify about him that everyone who believes in him receives forgiveness of sins through his name. (Acts 10:43)

To gain context on this verse, read Acts 10:23-48.

The prophets made some pretty incredible statements about Jesus. Many of them said these things a thousand years before Jesus was born. Look up the following verses. What do they foretell of Jesus' life?

- Micah 5:2:

- Zechariah 9:9:

- Psalm 22:16:

What does Acts 10:43 say about forgiveness? How do we receive it?

Believe can be a difficult word to live out.

There's an old story of a daredevil who pushed a wheelbarrow across a tightrope over Niagara Falls. Crowds watched from the sides as the daredevil pushed the wheelbarrow across. Many didn't believe it could be done until they saw it.

Next, the man put one hundred pounds of stones in the wheelbarrow. Again the crowd didn't believe he could push it across until they saw him do it.

Finally, having pushed the wheelbarrow across and back with a 150-pound load, the daredevil asked for a volunteer to get into the wheelbarrow for the trip. There were no takers. To take that offer would require incredible belief, even in the face of having seen it done.

We receive eternal life through our belief in Jesus Christ. We haven't actually seen Him in person, but we are asked to get into the wheelbarrow.

How can you increase your belief in Jesus Christ? Where is He asking you to step out in faith today?

THE COST OF FORGIVENESS

He was pierced for our transgressions,
he was crushed for our iniquities;
the punishment that brought us peace was upon him,
and by his wounds we are healed. (Isaiah 53:5)

As said above, there were many prophecies about Jesus. One of the most incredible prophecies comes from Isaiah 53. Read that chapter.

What did the prophet Isaiah say about Jesus in the following verses of chapter 53?

- Verse 3:

- Verse 5:

- Verse 6:

- Verse 7:

- Verse 9:

- Verse 12:

How was Jesus "pierced for our transgressions"? (Try to get beyond just the physical aspects of this answer.)

Isaiah 53:5 uses two words for why Jesus went to the cross. They are two words that describe our condition. What are they?

1.

2.

The verse then uses two words to describe our current condition, our new life in Christ. What are they?

1.

2.

Isaiah 53 does not paint a pretty picture of Jesus, the life He lived, or our condition. As ugly as the picture may be, though, the outcome is beautiful.

DEATH TO SIN

He himself bore our sins in his body on the tree, so that we might die to sins and live for righteousness; by his wounds you have been healed. (1 Peter 2:24)

Read 1 Peter 2:21-25.

Title this passage. What is the primary message?

How did Jesus model what it means to "live for righteousness"?

> For Jesus to save others, quite simply, he could not save
> himself. [1]
>
> —PHILIP YANCEY

Jesus took our sins upon Himself so that we may "die to sins and live for righteousness." How have you died to sins? How do you still have to die to sins?

In light of all that is being said here, what does it mean for you to "live for righteousness"?

BOUGHT BACK

In him we have redemption through his blood, the forgiveness of sins, in accordance with the riches of God's grace that he lavished on us with all wisdom and understanding. (Ephesians 1:7-8)

Begin by reading all of Ephesians 1. Ephesians 1:2 describes God as Father. This was a twist, as ancient gods were tyrants to be feared, not parents to be loved. Yet in this first chapter of Ephesians there are a number of words that might be associated with a family or acceptance into a family, such as "inheritance," "chose," and "adoption." Look through the chapter and note those words.

We have been adopted into God's family, and we have been redeemed. What does "redeem" mean?

How have we been redeemed?

What were we redeemed from?

God does not blindly give the gift of redemption like a rich uncle we hardly know who sends us lavish toys or hundred-dollar bills each Christmas and birthday. God lavishes us with _____ and _____.

He is smart and knows our situation, yet He still lavishes us with His grace. Incredible!

CHAPTER FOUR

ASSURANCE OF STRENGTH

There will be times of discouragement. There will be times when you feel weak. In those times, there is a resource that you can call on to give you strength.

The reality is that in Christ you are strong. God said,

"Do not fear, for I am with you . . .
I will strengthen you and help you;
    I will uphold you with my righteous right hand."
(Isaiah 41:10)

Fear God and thou shalt not quail before the terrors of men. [1]

—THOMAS À KEMPIS

In fact, God has promised you a victory. You are on the winning side. Even if you do experience a few losses, in the end you will win with Jesus.

So, "Be strong and courageous. Do not be terrified; do not be discouraged, for the LORD your God will be with you wherever you go" (Joshua 1:9). And memorize this:

- 1 Corinthians 15:56-57
- 2 Thessalonians 3:3
- John 10:10
- 2 Peter 1:3

VICTORY OVER DEATH

The sting of death is sin, and the power of sin is the law. But thanks be to God! He gives us the victory through our Lord Jesus Christ. (1 Corinthians 15:56-57)

The author of 1 Corinthians 15 wrote about the resurrection of Christ, the resurrection of the dead, and the resurrection body. To better understand these two verses, read the entire chapter.

"No fear" is a common saying today. But all of us have fear. What do you fear?

Do you fear death? If so, why?

Should you fear death? Why or why not?

Whether or not you fear death, you can be sure of this fact: the Lord Jesus Christ will give you victory in all things, including death.

SAFE FROM EVIL

The Lord is faithful, and he will strengthen and protect you from the evil one. (2 Thessalonians 3:3)

For context, read all of 2 Thessalonians 3.

What was the first request the author made to the Thessalonians in chapter 3?

What two things did the author want his readers to pray for?

1.

2.

The author made all of these requests based on verse 3. What was the basis of his request?

We all have a story about how we have seen evil in our school, our neighborhood, or our own heart. Where have you seen evil in your world or community?

Where have you seen evil in your school?

Where have you seen evil in your own life?

God will do two things for you in the face of evil. He will
_____ and _____ you.

Don't look for evil, but when you confront it, know that you have been given an opportunity to grow.

LIFE TO THE FULL

"The thief comes only to steal and kill and destroy; I have come that they may have life, and have it to the full." (John 10:10)

Read John 10:1-18. Jesus was making an exclusive claim in the form of a parable. (A parable is a story that makes a point.)

Where was Jesus telling this parable? (You may need to go back a few chapters to find the answer.)

To whom was Jesus telling this parable?

The story Jesus told contains a few characters. The first is the thief. He is also called a _____.

The story also mentions sheep. Who do the sheep in the parable represent?

Another character is the hired hand. When danger comes, what does the hired hand do?

Who does the hired hand represent?

Of course the shepherd is Jesus. What do you learn about Jesus from this parable?

Many people think that a life with Christ is a mediocre life. The reality, though, is that Jesus promises us not only life, but life to the full.

POWER AND PROVISION

His divine power has given us everything we need for life and godliness through our knowledge of him who called us by his own glory and goodness. (2 Peter 1:3)

Begin by reading 2 Peter 1:3-12.

If your Bible has section titles, what is the title for this section of Scripture? If it does not, make up your own title.

God's divine power has given us everything we need for
_____ and _____.

How would God provide everything you need for life? What has He provided for your life already?

How would God provide everything you need for godliness? What has He provided for your godliness already?

We do not receive power from God because we go to church, stay in school, or don't do drugs. We receive all that we do out of God's own _____ and _____.

CHAPTER FIVE

ASSURANCE OF AN ANSWER

In your life journey with Christ there will not only be times of attack, but there will also be times when you feel abandoned.

Sometimes you may think that God is not listening. You may believe that you are on your own or that no help is available.

But you are not alone on this life journey. With Christ, you have direct access to God, including the ability to talk to Him at any point. And not only can you talk to Him, but most importantly, He will listen.

> *When we pray, genuinely pray, the real condition of our heart is revealed. This is as it should be. This is when God truly begins to work with us. The adventure is just beginning.*[1]
>
> —RICHARD J. FOSTER

God wants you to talk to Him about everything, and He promises an answer. So memorize this:

- John 16:24
- Matthew 7:7-8
- Jeremiah 33:3
- 1 John 5:14

INVITATION TO ASK

"Until now you have not asked for anything in my name. Ask and you will receive, and your joy will be complete." (John 16:24)

Read John 16 in its entirety.

What is the context for John 16:24? What was about to happen to Jesus? What was Jesus talking about in this section?

When making a request to God, whose name should you use?

What would you like to ask God for that you have not yet asked?

Why haven't you asked?

What hurdles need to be removed for you to feel free to ask?

When you pray, what should you expect?

PROMISE OF AN ANSWER

"Ask and it will be given to you; seek and you will find; knock and the door will be opened to you. For everyone who asks receives; he who seeks finds; and to him who knocks, the door will be opened." (Matthew 7:7-8)

Read chapters 5–7 in the gospel of Matthew.

Where was Jesus speaking and to whom was He speaking in Matthew 7:7-8?

These verses run on two tracks of three.

The first track, made up of the first sentence, is this:

- "Ask and it will be _____."
- "Seek and you will _____."
- "Knock and the door will be _____."

The second track, made up of the second sentence, is this:

- "Everyone who asks _____."
- "He who seeks _____."
- "To him who knocks, the door will be _____."

Do you see the parallels in this passage? Take note of parallels in the Bible. They show that the writer was making a point.

Take a few minutes to work through these two tracks of thinking. What do you learn from the parallels found in this passage?

MORE THAN WE COULD IMAGINE

"Call to me and I will answer you and tell you great and unsearchable things you do not know." (Jeremiah 33:3)

Read all of Jeremiah 33. As we have explored these Bible passages, we have seen this again and again: God doesn't merely meet our needs; He goes beyond our needs and even our expectations.

According to the memory verse, if you call on God, what will He do?

He will not only answer you but will also tell you _____
and _____ things.

We may understand "great things," but what are "unsearchable" things?

Take some time to dream with God. What are the "great and
unsearchable things" that you do not know but that God may want
you to explore with Him?

PRAYER AND GOD'S WILL

> This is the confidence we have in approaching God: that if
> we ask anything according to his will, he hears us.
> (1 John 5:14)

Read 1 John 5.

There is a twist in 1 John 5:14 compared to the other three verses in
this section. What is it?

What is meant by God's will?

God can answer our prayer requests in three ways: "go," "no," or "slow." How do you think God would respond if you asked for something He knew was not good for you?

Have you ever had an experience when God said "no"? If so, describe it.

Although God's refusal may have been a disappointment, does hindsight allow you to see His reasoning for saying no? If so, what was it?

Sometimes what we ask for is not the wrong thing, but it is the wrong time. In times like this, God's answer is "slow." He asks us to wait. Has there been a time when you asked God for something and it took Him a long time to answer you? What was that experience like?

When the time is right and the request is good, we get a "go" response from God. This occurs when we ask according to His will. Take note when this happens in your life. Do you have an example of when God said "go"?

CHAPTER SIX

ASSURANCE OF ETERNAL LIFE

A bank recently opened in our town. In front of the newly con-
structed building was a large sign that said, "This is how you get
there." When I saw the sign, I thought, *Get where? To the bank? I have
to stand in front of the bank to see the sign.*

Obviously, the sign was talking about something other than a
location. It was talking about a place in life. The "there" stood for
intangible ideas such as contentment, peace, success, and so on.
That is what the world is after, and most people are expecting to
"get there" through good management of their financial affairs.

The good news is that Jesus offers us contentment and peace
and success—and more. He also gives us eternal life. Our "there"
isn't actually in this world. It is in our eternal existence with Jesus.
While Jesus will give us all we need for this life, that doesn't compare to what He will give us in eternal life.

Memorize this and you will have greater assurance of your
eternal life:

- 1 John 5:11-12
- Hebrews 2:14-15
- John 3:16
- 1 John 2:17

LIFE IN THE SON

This is the testimony: God has given us eternal life, and this life is in his Son. He who has the Son has life; he who does not have the Son of God does not have life. (1 John 5:11-12)

In chapter 5, you read all of 1 John 5. For this memory verse, focus on verses 1-12 of 1 John 5.

Does your Bible have a title for this passage? If so, what is it?

This passage has a great deal for us to learn about our life journey. What do you learn from the following verses?

• Verse 2:

• Verses 4-5:

• Verse 9:

• Verse 10:

Does your salvation come from what you do on a daily basis? Why or why not?

Who gives us eternal life?

LIEUTENANT DAN: "Have you found God yet, Gump?"
FORREST: "I didn't know that I was supposed to be looking for him."

—FORREST GUMP

We find in this verse a dividing line. Those who have Christ have
_____. Those who do not have Christ do
not have _____.

What does this mean for you and your friends?

FREEDOM FROM FEAR OF DEATH

Since the children have flesh and blood, he too shared in their humanity so that by his death he might destroy him who holds the power of death — that is, the devil — and free those who all their lives were held in slavery by their fear of death. (Hebrews 2:14-15)

To gain context on these verses, read all of Hebrews 2.

What insights do you gain from the following verses?

- Verse 1:

- Verse 10:

- Verse 11:

Why did God's Son become a human being, according to Hebrews 2:14-15?

Who did Jesus destroy by His death?

What does this mean for you?

Hebrews 2:14-15 says that we are held in slavery by a fear of death. What else holds you in slavery? That is, what else do you fear?

Having been released from slavery, how can you live differently in the world?

> *I am increasingly convinced that conversion is the individual*
> *equivalent of revolution.* [1]
>
> —HENRI J. M. NOUWEN

LIFE THROUGH BELIEF

"God so loved the world that he gave his one and only Son, that whoever believes in him shall not perish but have eternal life." (John 3:16)

This verse is part of Jesus' conversation with Nicodemus, a religious leader. Read John 3:1-21.

John 3:16 is not only one of the most familiar and memorized verses in the Bible, but it is also one of the most powerful. Hopefully, it is a slam dunk to your soul near the end of this first *Memorize This* stage.

What did God's love cause Him to do?

John 3:16 says that God gave "his one and only Son." What does it mean that He gave His Son?

How do you think God expects us to react to this gift?

What do those who believe in the Son receive?

Read 1 John 4:9-10. How is this passage similar to John 3:16?

What new insights can you find in the passage from 1 John?

What do you expect eternal life to be like? Take a few minutes to imagine it, and then do one of the following: draw a picture of what heaven may look like or write a poem about eternal life.

HOW TO LIVE FOREVER

The world and its desires pass away, but the man who does the will of God lives forever. (1 John 2:17)

For context, read 1 John 2:1-17.

The Bible often talks about "the world." To what is it referring?

How do you experience "the world" in your daily life?

What are some of your "worldly desires"? In other words, what are some things in the world you long for? (Be honest!)

An old bumper sticker says, "He who dies with the most toys wins." According to 1 John 2:17, is that true or false?

What actually happens to all of those "toys"?

1 John 2:17 tells us there is one thing that will last forever. What is it?

How can you and your friends do the will of God today?

CHAPTER SEVEN

ASSURANCE OF GUIDANCE

As you pursue the Lord, there will be challenges and frustrations. There will be times when you need to cry out to Him in prayer. Finally, there will be times when you need guidance. You might ask, *Where should I go to college? Which ministry should I get involved in? Who should I marry?* "God, what is Your will?" is a common cry.

You can look to the Lord for guidance, direction, and purpose for your life. He is ready and willing to provide.

Memorize this and you will grow in your assurance of God's guidance:

- Proverbs 3:5-6
- Psalm 32:8
- Jeremiah 17:7
- 1 John 4:4

THE IMPORTANCE OF TRUST

Trust in the LORD with all your heart
    and lean not on your own understanding;
in all your ways acknowledge him,
    and he will make your paths straight. (Proverbs 3:5-6)

Read Proverbs 3.

You are probably familiar with the word *proverb* from its use with Chinese proverbs. Biblical proverbs aren't much different in format.

In general, the book of Proverbs offers a number of brief insights into our spiritual journey. They could be called Bible McNuggets. They are short and tasty little truths from the Word of God.

As stated in Proverbs 3:5-6, who are we to trust?

How are we to trust in Him?

When you find yourself not trusting God, who are you usually trusting instead?

These verses ask us to acknowledge God in all our ways. How can you do that?

> *The mission is God's. We are joining in with God's activity, not God with ours. . . . To forget this is to make our practice an idol. God becomes controlled by our programs and expectations and thus no god at all.* [1]
>
> —PETE WARD

The amazing truth of these verses is found in the last little nugget: "He will make your paths straight." It doesn't say, "He may make your paths straight" or "He will make your paths less curvy." God will make your way straight.

SOMEONE TO WATCH OVER US

I will instruct you and teach you in the way you should go;
I will counsel you and watch over you. (Psalm 32:8)

Remember that psalms are prayers, poems, and songs sung to God. Pray Psalm 32 to God.

What insights did you gain by praying this psalm?

Who is blessed, according to verses 1 and 2?

What happens to your sin when you confess it to God, according to verse 5?

What did you learn from verse 7?

What can you expect from God, according to verse 10?

Finally, write your own version of this psalm. Follow the same themes verse by verse, but include your own words, examples, and experiences.

CONFIDENCE IN GOD

"Blessed is the man who trusts in the LORD,
    whose confidence is in him." (Jeremiah 17:7)

For context, read Jeremiah 17:5-18.

What does it mean to be blessed?

What does it mean to trust in God?

How do you trust in God today?

Is there a person in whom you have great confidence? Name him or her.

What gives you confidence in this person?

Draw comparisons and contrasts between your experiences with that person and your experiences with God.

How can you have more confidence in God?

Activities like climbing, rappelling, zip lines, and rope courses are thrilling. I do not like the heights these activities involve, but I often find myself doing them with a group of students.

One time I went on a giant swing called "The Silencer." It was called "The Silencer" because it had such a tremendous fall that those on it couldn't even manage a scream through their fear. The people working "The Silencer" were in Hawaiian costumes, telling jokes and laughing. I was about to trust my life to them, and they seemed to have no regard for the responsibility they were taking on. I'm sure they were a fun group, but I wanted people I could trust.

The God we serve is like those workers in that He is full of fun and excitement. But when it comes to the "fall," we can trust that He is ready and prepared to catch us.

OVERCOMING THE WORLD

> You, dear children, are from God and have overcome them,
> because the one who is in you is greater than the one who is
> in the world. (1 John 4:4)

To gain context, read 1 John 4 in its entirety.

In the memory verse, we are referred to as "dear children." And we are
not just children, but *victorious* children, of God. What does that mean?

This verse has three unnamed players. The first is the "them" whom
we have "overcome." Who is it that we have "overcome"?

Now that we've defined "them," who is the "one who is in you"?

Finally, who is this "one who is in the world"?

Now that you have all the definitions, rewrite this verse with the characters in place.

How has this verse been true in your life?

You have completed the first set of verses in *Memorize This*. Congratulations! You deserve praise, as this has been a big task.

In school you have an obvious progression. If you pass seventh grade, you advance to eighth grade. When you graduate from high school, you move on to college or a job. Yet in our life journey with Christ, we do not often have natural progressions and opportunities to celebrate.

Well, here is an opportunity for you to celebrate. You have done very well and are graduating to the next level. Take an opportunity to celebrate what you have accomplished.

GROWING DISCIPLE

To be a disciple means to be a student. At this point in your life journey with Jesus, it is critical that you see yourself as a student. The journey is not over. It is only beginning.

You are growing in your faith with the help of many sources at this point. God, Jesus, the Bible, and many people in your life are all teaching you.

In addition, you should be learning on your own as you become not only a disciple *of* Jesus but also a disciple *for* Jesus. You will continue to learn and grow as you become an active presence of Jesus among the people you know and upon this earth.

CHAPTER EIGHT

DISCIPLE OF GOD

God calls us to be His disciples first and foremost. We should seek to follow Him with all we've got.

We need to recognize that God is our teacher. It is easy at times to see Jesus as our teacher or to see the people teaching us today, but God as our teacher? Yes.

> *When thou hast read and learned many things, thou must always return to one first principle. I am He that teaches man knowledge.* [1]

—THOMAS À KEMPIS

Memorize this and you will be a disciple of God:

- Matthew 22:37
- Deuteronomy 7:9
- 1 Corinthians 10:31
- 1 Chronicles 29:11

LOVING GOD

"'Love the Lord your God with all your heart and with all your soul and with all your mind.'" (Matthew 22:37)

For context, read Matthew 22:34-40. Jesus was quoting an Old Testament passage in Matthew 22:37. For more context, read Deuteronomy 6:5-6.

From the Deuteronomy passage, where are we supposed to keep this command?

According to the memory passage, we are to love God with three things. What are they?

1.

2.

3.

What does it mean to love God "with all your heart"?

What does it mean to love God "with all your soul"?

Finally, what does it mean to love God "with all your mind"?

THE FAITHFULNESS OF GOD

Know therefore that the LORD your God is God; he is the faithful God, keeping his covenant of love to a thousand generations of those who love him and keep his commands. (Deuteronomy 7:9)

Read Deuteronomy 7 to gain a sense of the context.

The psalms speak to God's faithfulness. Look up the following verses from Psalms. What do you learn about faithfulness from each one?

• Psalm 18:25:

• Psalm 33:4:

• Psalm 108:4:

• Psalm 145:13:

• Psalm 146:6:

How would you define faithfulness in light of your own experiences, Deuteronomy 7:9, and these psalms?

How has God been faithful to you?

How has God been faithful to your family?

What does it mean for you to "love him and keep his commands" (Deuteronomy 7:9)?

ALL FOR GOD'S GLORY

> Whether you eat or drink or whatever you do, do it all for the glory of God. (1 Corinthians 10:31)

To gain understanding through context, read 1 Corinthians 10:23–11:1.

What does 1 Corinthians 10:31 suggest should we should do for the glory of God?

According to Colossians 3:17, what should be done for the glory of God?

Read 1 Peter 4:11. What does this verse say should be done to the glory of God?

Eating, drinking, speaking, doing, serving—what does it mean to perform these actions to the glory of God?

How can you be more deliberate as a disciple of God today?

KINGLY POWER

> Yours, O LORD, is the greatness and the power
> > and the glory and the majesty and the splendor,
> > for everything in heaven and earth is yours.
> Yours, O LORD, is the kingdom;
> > you are exalted as head over all. (1 Chronicles 29:11)

Read 1 Chronicles 29:1-20 for context.

The psalms talk not only about God's faithfulness but also about His power. Read the following verses. What do you learn about God's power from each one?

- Psalm 24:8:

- Psalm 59:17:

- Psalm 62:11:

Greatness, power, glory, and majesty—what do those words mean to you?

What do they mean when they are used together?

What does it mean in your life that God is "head over all"?

CHAPTER NINE

DISCIPLE OF CHRIST

Jesus was called a teacher. While we may struggle with the idea of being a disciple of God, being a disciple of Jesus is a common thought.

Jesus Himself would respond to the title "Teacher." John 13:13 quotes Christ as saying, "You call me 'Teacher' and 'Lord,' and rightly so, for that is what I am." In fact, He is the greatest teacher who has ever lived.

We are called to be Christ's ambassadors, learning from Him and teaching the world. Memorize this and you will be a greater disciple of Christ:

- 1 John 2:6
- 1 Corinthians 15:22
- Philippians 2:10-11
- Colossians 2:6

THE JESUS WALK

Whoever claims to live in him must walk as Jesus did.
(1 John 2:6)

Read 1 John 1:5–2:14.

What does your Bible title this section? What would you title this section?

Have you ever had to walk in a dark, scary place (maybe an alley or a cave)? Describe that experience. What did it feel like?

We are encouraged to walk in the light. What does it mean, practically, to walk in the light?

What does it mean to walk in darkness?

The word "claim" is used five times in this passage, four times negatively and once positively.

What are the negative claims in these verses?

- 1 John 1:6:

- 1 John 1:8:

- 1 John 1:10:

- 1 John 2:9:

What is the positive claim of this passage? (See 1 John 2:6.)

What does it mean to "walk as Jesus did"?

> *His appearance in our midst has made it undeniably clear that changing the human heart and changing human society are not separate tasks, but are as interconnected as the two beams of the cross.*[1]
>
> —HENRI J. M. NOUWEN

ALIVE IN CHRIST

As in Adam all die, so in Christ all will be made alive. (1 Corinthians 15:22)

> *Because we children of Adam want to become great,*
>   *He became small.*
> *Because we will not stoop,*
>   *He humbled himself.*
> *Because we want to rule,*
>   *He came to serve.*[2]
>
> —J. OSWALD SANDERS

You've previously read 1 Corinthians 15 in this study, but it's worth reading again.

Who was Adam?

Why is his death significant for you?

Adam was the first to sin. How does that impact you?

How are all "made alive" in Christ?

Draw a model, framework, or flowchart to explain the relationship among Adam, Christ, and you. Be creative.

ON BENDED KNEE

> At the name of Jesus every knee should bow,
>   in heaven and on earth and under the earth,
> and every tongue confess that Jesus Christ is Lord,
>   to the glory of God the Father. (Philippians 2:10-11)

Read Philippians 2:5-11.

What should your attitude be?

How was Jesus "in very nature God"? (verse 6)

In what way did Jesus make "himself nothing"? (verse 7)

How did Jesus humble Himself?

How (if at all) do the last three answers change your answer to the first question, "What should your attitude be?"

When reading the Bible, if you see the word "therefore," you need to ask, "What is it there for?" What is the "therefore" at the beginning of verse 9 there for?

What is the "highest place"? (verse 9)

What is the response to the name Jesus?

Where does that response occur?

What is your part in this passage?

CONTINUING IN JESUS

Just as you received Christ Jesus as Lord, continue to live in him. (Colossians 2:6)

For context, read Colossians 1:24–2:23.

I can remember the summer evening when I went forward to make a personal commitment to Jesus Christ. I was seven years old, and it was on the last night of a week-long, family Bible camp.

I'm not sure who the speaker was, nor am I sure of what was shared, but I am convinced that I met God that night. It was a life-changing experience, and I came home excited about my newfound faith.

From that point forward, there came a number of peaks and valleys in my life journey with Jesus. I'd go to the Dunes for a youth retreat and return home ready to take on the world, only to find myself not living for the Lord by the end of second period on Monday.

What has the journey been like for you? When and how did you receive Jesus Christ as Lord?

What were your emotions during that time?

During the months that followed, what were your experiences with Christ like?

How can you continue to have a connection with Jesus as you did at first?

I want a lifetime of holy moments. Every day I want to be in dangerous proximity to Jesus. [3]

—MICHAEL YACONELLI

CHAPTER TEN

DISCIPLE OF THE WORD

One of the primary ways we are able to be disciples of God and Jesus is through the Word of God, the Bible. It is a critical component in the life journey of Christ's followers. It is also critical to our ability to lead and witness to those around us.

The Bible should be a major part of your life as you move through the day. When you are faced with a challenge, the challenges faced by people in the Bible should encourage you. When you are tempted, you should remember that Jesus was also tempted and used the Bible as a defense. It is in these situations that you are a disciple of the Word. By putting it to use, you are testifying to its power and prominence in your life.

In your life journey, you will have special opportunities to talk with someone about Jesus. You may even have an opportunity to lead someone to commit his or her life to Christ. It is in these times that you will want to share the Word of God. In these God-ordained meetings, you will be glad that you memorized this:

- Colossians 3:16
- Romans 15:4
- Deuteronomy 11:18-19
- James 1:22

THE INDWELLING WORD

Let the word of Christ dwell in you richly as you teach and admonish one another with all wisdom, and as you

sing psalms, hymns and spiritual songs with gratitude in your
hearts to God. (Colossians 3:16)

Read Colossians 3 for context.

What is the "word of Christ"?

What does it mean for the word of Christ to "dwell in you richly"?

Have you had opportunities to teach? When? Who?

How have you used the Bible in those opportunities?

What does it mean to "admonish"?

How do you use the Bible to admonish without being harsh or
destructive?

Do you sing any worship songs or hymns that include Bible verses? If
so, name some of them.

Have you had a time of worship with gratitude in your heart and another time without it? How did you know the difference?

ENCOURAGEMENT FROM THE WORD

Everything that was written in the past was written to teach us, so that through endurance and the encouragement of the Scriptures we might have hope. (Romans 15:4)

Read Romans 14:1–15:13.

Was this book written before, during, or after the life of Christ?

According to the memory verse, we have hope for our life with Christ, not in the Scriptures alone, but also through endurance. What does this mean?

How have the Scriptures helped you endure hard times?

How have hard times helped you understand Scripture?

IN TOUCH WITH THE WORD

> Fix these words of mine in your hearts and minds; tie them as
> symbols on your hands and bind them on your foreheads.
> Teach them to your children, talking about them when you sit
> at home and when you walk along the road, when you lie
> down and when you get up. (Deuteronomy 11:18-19)

I took a couple years of high school German. My buddies and I spent hours memorizing the vocabulary, the various forms of the definite article, and so forth. We could pass the test because we had fixed the words in our minds.

Then I had the chance to take a trip to Germany. At one of my first opportunities, I used one of my German lines. *I memorized the vocab. I can talk to these people,* I thought. In German, I asked a store clerk, "What is this?" She responded with a two- to three-minute description. I was lost from the first word. I still have no idea what she said.

There is a big difference between "knowing the vocab" and actually being able to converse in the language. The same is true of the Bible. You can have all of these verses memorized verbatim, backward, forward, and upside down, but if you don't put them to use, if they don't impact your life, if you don't share them with other people, then what is the use?

Read Deuteronomy 11:16-25.

What are "these words of mine"?

You are working to fix the Bible in your heart and mind by doing this project. Verse 18 uses figurative statements to illustrate what it means to know and use the words of the Bible. In a figurative sense, what does it mean to "tie them as symbols on your hands"?

What does it mean to "bind them on your foreheads"?

How did your parents or the person who helped lead you to Christ teach you the Bible?

According to this passage, how should you teach your future children (if any) about the Bible?

OBEDIENCE TO THE WORD

> Do not merely listen to the word, and so deceive yourselves. Do what it says. (James 1:22)

To learn more about listening and doing, read James 1:19-27.

What is the difference between listening and hearing?

Where do you listen to the Word of God?

What was the best scriptural sermon you ever heard? Why?

For you, what is a positive environment in which to hear the Word of God?

Do you have an example of when you really "heard" the Word of God? When and where was it? What happened?

In a sense, Nike didn't come up with the catchphrase "Just do it." Something similar is found right here in James 1:22: "Do what it says." Jesus made the same point in Matthew 7:21. What can we learn from these two verses?

Why is it important that we actually act upon what we hear?

CHAPTER ELEVEN

DISCIPLE OF OTHERS

You have now seen that we are disciples of God, of Jesus, and of the Bible. In addition, God expects us to be students, or disciples, of other people. God puts us into a community, and we learn and grow within that community.

This means that we should be part of a church—not only a youth group or Bible study, but also a regular worship and study experience attended by people of all ages. Do not dismiss the importance of being an active member of your church. The church has been called the bride of Christ, and a bride is important.

From a church community should arise other opportunities for instruction. You may be part of a small group at your church or school or in your neighborhood. You may want to work with other followers of Christ in your community to reach people who do not go to church. You may want to serve the less fortunate in your community because of your commitment to Christ. All of these are incredible opportunities for instruction. But no matter how or where you find it, you should receive more instruction than just what you get on Sunday morning from the pulpit.

> *Serving and suffering are paired in the teaching and life of our Lord. One does not come without the other.* [1]
>
> —J. OSWALD SANDERS

In addition to these examples, you should have a mentor or coach who is helping you learn. I hope this book has encouraged you to develop this important relationship. You should go through this chapter especially with a mentor.

It is important to realize that someone is always teaching you something. Class is always on. Look around you—you are the disciple of many people. Don't miss what God is teaching you through these people.

Memorize this and you will see that you are a disciple of others:

- Psalm 122:1
- Ecclesiastes 4:9-10
- Romans 12:4-5
- Proverbs 19:20

WORSHIPING WITH OTHERS

I rejoiced with those who said to me,
    "Let us go to the house of the LORD." (Psalm 122:1)

Read Psalm 122.

Are you usually excited about going to church? Why or why not?

What would it take to make you really excited about going to church?

What can you do to make that happen?

In Psalm 122:1, does the writer rejoice about going to church alone?

Who do you rejoice in seeing at church?

What does it mean that church is the "house of the LORD"?

How can you ensure that your church remains the "house of the LORD"?

People assemble for worship because God called them together whether they know it or not.[2]

—EUGENE PETERSON

THE BEAUTY OF COMMUNITY

Two are better than one,
    because they have a good return for their work:
If one falls down,
    his friend can help him up.
But pity the man who falls
    and has no one to help him up! (Ecclesiastes 4:9-10)

The fourth chapter of Ecclesiastes speaks of oppression, toil, and friendlessness. Read the chapter for a greater understanding of this verse.

A number of years ago there was a television show called the *A-Team*. (You may have seen reruns on cable.) One of the main characters, tough guy Mr. T, would clench his teeth, flex his muscles, and say, "I pity the fool." So does God. He pities those people who go it alone. God may say, "I pity the loner."

God doesn't want us to be alone. He wants us to work in community. That's why He's given us a church, small groups, and friends.

What is the answer to one plus one? Did you answer, "two"? Everyone knows that as a math equation, one plus one equals two, but as a people equation, one plus one is more than two.

Think of two people operating alone. What they can accomplish separately is not near what they can accomplish by working together. One person working with another person can equal power and strength that is greater than two.

Do you have someone you really like to work with (maybe somebody at work or a person you completed a project with at school)? Name him or her.

Why do you like working with this person?

What were you able to accomplish together compared to what you would have accomplished separately?

How did the other person help you?

How did you help your partner?

God says, "Pity the person who goes it privately, but praise the person who goes with a party." Who is helping you today in your walk with Christ? Who is there to pick you up when you fall?

Persons in the Fellowship are related to one another through Him, as all mountains go down into the same earth.[3]

—THOMAS KELLY

INTERDEPENDENCY

Just as each of us has one body with many members, and these members do not all have the same function, so in Christ we who are many form one body, and each member belongs to all the others. (Romans 12:4-5)

Read Romans 12:1-8 for context.

Name a few parts of your body.

What do those parts of your body do for you?

Name some members of your youth group or faith community.

What talents or gifts do those people bring to the group? (Maybe they play drums, are funny, or offer insightful comments.)

Identify one of the persons from your list. What would your group be like if everyone was like that person?

What are some headaches that come with having different people in your group?

What are some benefits to this variety?

Why do you think God made us all different?

How can you more easily recognize the way God is working in your midst through the makeup of your group?

GOOD ADVICE ABOUT ADVICE

> Listen to advice and accept instruction,
>   and in the end you will be wise. (Proverbs 19:20)

So that this verse does not live in isolation, read all of Proverbs 19.

Who has given you really good advice?

How do you know it was good advice?

Who is your favorite teacher?

Why is he or she a good instructor?

Read Proverbs 4:1. According to this verse, from whom should you accept instruction?

Read Proverbs 12:15. How does this verse affirm Proverbs 19:20?

What will happen if you "listen to advice and accept instruction"?

CHAPTER TWELVE

DISCIPLE OF LIFE

A line of clothing uses the slogan "Life is good." And it's true. Life *is* good. In fact, life is very good—even absolutely incredible—with Jesus.

God wants us to know Him, know the Word, and know His Son, and He wants us to know it all in this life. We don't learn all of that to sit in our little Christian circles and say, "Yippee!" We learn to use it in life.

This world isn't a mistake—it's God's creation for you. Enjoy it. And always be learning from your experiences. Life is a string of teachable moments.

> *Every man dies. Not every man really lives.*
>
> —WILLIAM WALLACE IN *BRAVEHEART*

Memorize this for a life that is good:

- Deuteronomy 26:16
- 1 Timothy 4:8
- Colossians 3:23
- 1 Corinthians 9:24

OBEDIENCE NOW

The LORD your God commands you this day to follow these decrees and laws; carefully observe them with all your heart and with all your soul. (Deuteronomy 26:16)

Deuteronomy 26 is about the commandment to tithe. Read the chapter for a greater understanding of this verse.

When was the last time you were commanded to do something?

What was it?

What was your response?

What does God command you to do?

Where do you find God's decrees and laws?

What does it mean to observe God's decrees and laws "with all your heart and with all your soul"?

When are you supposed to follow this command?

The memory verse says God commands us "this day" to follow His decrees. Why do you think there is an urgency to following God's commands?

SPIRITUAL EXERCISE

> Physical training is of some value, but godliness has value for all things, holding promise for both the present life and the life to come. (1 Timothy 4:8)

The book of 1 Timothy is a letter from Paul to Timothy. Chapter 4 of the book contains special instructions to Timothy. Read this chapter.

What activities do you do for physical exercise?

How do you feel, physically and emotionally, after you work out?

How is physical training limited as compared to spiritual training?

What things do you do for spiritual training?

How do you feel after you "work out" spiritually?

How does your spiritual training hold promise for "the present life"?

How does it hold promise for "the life to come"?

WHOLEHEARTED

Whatever you do, work at it with all your heart, as working for the Lord, not for men. (Colossians 3:23)

The third chapter in the book of Colossians is about rules for holy living. With this in mind, read the chapter to gain context on this verse.

Growing up in western Washington, we had a backyard full of weeds. The good soil and plentiful rain meant everything grew at will.

Rather than try to pull up all the weeds and plant grass, we mowed the weeds to look like a lawn. It was my job to mow the weeds. It was an awful job. Rocks flew out from below the mower, all kinds of weed clippings and dandelion leaves would billow around near the ground, and the kicker was the steep slope of the yard.

I hated mowing that yard. In fact, I hated it so much that I didn't mow it often. The result was that the weeds would get taller, and it would be an even more difficult job the next time.

My parents asked me to do this job, but I didn't want to do it. Then my youth group leader asked me to take another look at it. "Instead of mowing the yard for your parents or even so that you'll have a nice-looking yard," my leader asked, "what if you mowed the lawn for God?"

That question changed my perspective. Now I was mowing to please God. I was mowing the yard because I knew it would make Him happy if I obeyed my parents.

Judging by Colossians 3:23, would you say there are some things we should do for God and other things we do just for ourselves, or is everything done for God?

What does it mean to work at something "with all your heart"?

Is there a job or task that you just don't like to do?

How would that change if you did it for God instead of for whomever is asking you to do it?

Do you have to be employed by a church to work for God?

What are some things you would like to do when you are done with school?

What would it mean to do those things for God?

FINISHING WELL

> Do you not know that in a race all the runners run, but only one gets the prize? Run in such a way as to get the prize.
> (1 Corinthians 9:24)

Read 1 Corinthians 9 for context.

I coached high school football for years at Meadowdale High School in suburban Seattle. We had a pretty good football program. Many years, we finished second or third in the conference, and we even made the state playoffs one year.

Yet if you asked the students at Meadowdale, they'd say the football program was no good. We were constantly in the running but never won the conference title; therefore, people thought we stank.

The difference between first and second and between second and third is the same numerically, but emotionally the difference is not the same at all. Whether you finished second or third doesn't matter. Either way, you didn't win.

Have you ever finished second at some kind of contest? If so, describe it.

What did it feel like?

Have you ever finished first at something? If you have, what was it? Write about your experience.

What did that feel like?

Compare and contrast the two experiences.

Where does God want us to finish in the "race" that is the Christian life?

What is the "prize"?

What do you have to do to finish first?

CHAPTER THIRTEEN

DISCIPLE FOR CHRIST

A substantial part of learning is doing. You can listen to a talk about how to drive a car, but until you actually do it, you don't know what it's really like. It is in actually driving that you learn what it feels like to brake, to turn a corner, or to shift gears.

You have been called to be a disciple for Christ. This means you are His advocate for His work in this world. And it is in being His disciple that you will learn even more about what it means to follow Him.

Memorize this and go get 'em:

- 1 John 3:18
- 1 Corinthians 2:4-5
- Colossians 4:5
- 1 Timothy 4:12

LOVE IN DEEDS

Dear children, let us not love with words or tongue but with actions and in truth. (1 John 3:18)

Love for one another is the theme of 1 John 3:11-24. Read it for context on this verse.

How do you show love to your parents or a special friend?

What does it mean to "not love with words or tongue"?

Our greatest fulfillment lies in giving ourselves to others. [1]

—HENRI J. M. NOUWEN

Read Ezekiel 33:30-32. What do you learn about how you should love God from those verses?

What does it mean to love "with actions"?

What does it mean to love "in truth"?

Read Romans 12:9. How does that enhance your understanding of loving "in truth"?

How can you improve in your ability to love "with actions and in truth"?

WISE FOOLS

> My message and my preaching were not with wise and persuasive words, but with a demonstration of the Spirit's power, so that your faith might not rest on men's wisdom, but on God's power. (1 Corinthians 2:4-5)

Read 1 Corinthians 1:18–2:5.

What does your Bible title this section? (If your Bible does not have section titles, create one.)

The message of Christ can have two responses. What are they?

1.

2.

From this passage, what is foolishness according to God?

What is wisdom to God?

Have you ever learned from a smart and persuasive teacher? If so, what was that like?

Have you ever learned in a community where God seemed to be moving? How was that different from learning under the smart and persuasive teacher?

Why does 1 Corinthians 2:4 caution us about preaching "with wise and persuasive words"?

How can you ensure that people's faith will rest on God's power and not on the words you use?

DIPLOMATIC CONTACTS

> Be wise in the way you act toward outsiders; make the most of every opportunity. (Colossians 4:5)

For context, read Colossians 4:2-6.

We were just cautioned about wise words in the last verse. What does it mean to be wise in Colossians 4:5?

Who are "outsiders" in the context of this memory verse?

Who are some outsiders in your life?

In a practical sense, what does it mean for you to be wise toward outsiders?

How can you earn a right to be heard by them?

How do you balance being wise and making the most of every opportunity?

YOUNG AND EXEMPLARY

> Don't let anyone look down on you because you are young, but set an example for the believers in speech, in life, in love, in faith and in purity. (1 Timothy 4:12)

You read 1 Timothy 4 earlier in this study, but to refresh your memory for this verse, read it again.

Have you ever had someone look down on you because you are young? If so, what happened?

How did you feel about it?

What can you do to ensure that people do not look down on you because of your age?

Have you ever been a role model for someone (maybe a younger sibling or an underclassman)? If so, who was it?

How did you know you were a role model?

What did you do as a role model?

Who are we to set an example for, according to 1 Timothy 4:12?

How do we set an example "in speech"?

How do we set an example "in life"?

How do we set an example "in love"?

How do we set an example "in faith"?

How do we set an example "in purity"?

Who are some people you can be discipling for Christ right now?

What are you going to do this week to start?

You have now completed the second stage of *Memorize This*. Well done!

Take a moment to think back over all you have done and how you have grown as a disciple of Christ. If you are working with a mentor or partner or group, talk it over together. Then pick some way to celebrate your achievements so far.

LIFE ISSUES

Life is full of issues, especially for a young person. You have probably learned about yourself in relation to many issues of life as you have met with your mentor or small group and worked through the Growing Disciple verses.

In this section you will walk through a number of issues that are common to the maturing young follower of Christ. The life issues addressed in this section include:

- Love
- Prayer
- Purity
- Giving
- Humility
- Perseverance
- Study
- Worship

Some of these issues were covered in the first section when, as a new believer, you were introduced to these concepts. This section will seek to confirm what God is doing in these areas of your life.

Remember that the spiritual life is not a stagnant life. It is a life that is growing, changing, and maturing. You may grow out of some challenges, but you will grow into new challenges. Having the issues of this section under control in your spiritual life will give you a foundation to handle any challenges that come your way.

CHAPTER FOURTEEN

LOVE

Love can be difficult. There will be times when you won't want to love. There will be people you won't want to love. And there will be situations in which you won't be able to love.

God has called us to be more than people who are loving in certain situations; He has called us to *be* love. We are to be His shining lights of love in the world.

> *It is only when we have claimed our own place in God's love that we can experience this all-embracing, non-comparing love and feel safe, not only with God, but also with our brothers and sisters.* [1]
>
> —HENRI J. M. NOUWEN

Memorize this and you will shine the light of love brightly:

- James 1:19-20
- Psalm 89:1-2
- 1 John 4:11
- John 15:17

THE DANGER OF ANGER

My dear brothers, take note of this: Everyone should be quick to listen, slow to speak and slow to become angry, for man's anger does not bring about the righteous life that God desires. (James 1:19-20)

Read James 1 for context.

What does it mean to be "quick to listen" and "slow to speak"?

Is it difficult for you to listen? Why or why not?

> *Leaders who want to show sensitivity should listen often and long and talk short and seldom. True leaders know that time spent listening is well invested.*[2]
>
> —J. OSWALD SANDERS

How does being a good listener show love to the person who is speaking?

Practice good listening in your conversations this week. Come back afterward and write what you have learned about yourself.

What makes you really mad?

What does Matthew 5:22 say about anger?

What does James 1:20 say about it?

Tie listening and anger together. How do these two relate, in your experience?

IN PRAISE OF GOD'S LOVE

> I will sing of the LORD's great love forever;
> > with my mouth I will make your faithfulness known
> > through all generations.
> I will declare that your love stands firm forever,
> > that you established your faithfulness in heaven itself.
> > (Psalm 89:1-2)

For context, read Psalm 89.

Write a love song to the Lord about how He has cared for you. If you are not a songwriter, write a poem or a short story. Make sure you include the elements expressed in Psalm 89:1-2 (for example, how God has been faithful to you and your family). Share your creation with a friend.

What was it like to write a song or poem to God? Write about your experience.

SPREADING LOVE AROUND

Dear friends, since God so loved us, we also ought to love one another. (1 John 4:11)

You read all of 1 John 4 long ago in chapter 7. Read 1 John 4:7-21 to refresh your memory.

How many times is the name "God" used in this passage?

How many times is the word "love" used in this passage?

Where does love come from, according to verse 7?

What do you learn about love from verse 8?

What do you learn about God from verse 8?

What is love, according to verse 10?

Look at verses 11 and 19. Why should we love?

How is God's love made complete, as stated in verse 12?

From verse 18, answer this question: Can love and fear exist together? Why or why not?

> *No one can help anyone without becoming involved, without entering with his whole person into the painful situation, without taking the risk of becoming hurt.*[3]
>
> —HENRI J. M. NOUWEN

MUTUAL LOVE

"This is my command: Love each other." (John 15:17)

Read John 15:9-17. Look at verses 12 and 17. Do you see the similarity? These verses serve as bookends for a number of love principles that are included between them.

What do the following verses teach us about love?

- Verse 13:

- Verse 14:

- Verse 15:

- Verse 16:

Why is love a critical component for the follower of Christ?

CHAPTER FIFTEEN

PRAYER

Prayer is your opportunity to talk to God. For the follower of Christ, it is a rescue, a right, and a responsibility.

First, prayer is your life preserver. When you are in trouble, you can call out to God in prayer, and He will be there, ready and willing to rescue you.

Second, prayer is an incredible privilege. The fact that you get to talk to the Creator of the universe is an amazing opportunity. Take advantage of it. Prayer is your right as a follower of Jesus.

Third, prayer is your responsibility. God has called us to pray for the world. We are required to live up to that calling. Don't take lightly your responsibility to pray.

> *If prayer is silly or unnecessary, Jesus would not have wasted His time at it.* [1]
>
> —J. OSWALD SANDERS

Memorize this and prayer will become a more significant event in your life:

- Psalm 62:8
- 1 Samuel 12:23
- 1 Thessalonians 5:17-18
- Matthew 6:9-13

TRUSTING ALWAYS

> Trust in him at all times, O people;
>   pour out your hearts to him,
>   for God is our refuge. (Psalm 62:8)

For context, read Psalm 62.

When are you to trust in God?

Do you trust in God "at all times"? Why or why not?

Who is someone you have poured out your heart to?

Why did you pour out your heart to him or her?

What does it mean to pour out your heart to God?

Why are we to trust in God?

INTERCESSORY PRAYER

> As for me, far be it from me that I should sin against the LORD
> by failing to pray for you. And I will teach you the way that is
> good and right. (1 Samuel 12:23)

For context, read Samuel's farewell speech in 1 Samuel 12.

What did the following people ask God to provide, and for whom were they praying?

- Moses in Numbers 11:1-2:

- Samuel in 1 Samuel 7:7-9:

- Paul in Romans 1:8-10:

What do you learn about prayer from these verses?

We have a responsibility to pray for others. What happens if we do not pray?

Prayer is not our only task. Coupled with this call to pray is a second call (see 1 Samuel 12:23). What is it?

How do prayer and teaching go together?

UNCEASING PRAYER

Pray continually; give thanks in all circumstances, for this is
God's will for you in Christ Jesus. (1 Thessalonians 5:17-18)

Paul, the writer of 1 Thessalonians, was giving final instructions to the
church. Read 1 Thessalonians 5:12-28 for context.

Verse 17 commands us to "pray continually." This command is illus-
trated by a parable Jesus told in Luke 18:1-8. Read that parable and
record what light it sheds for you on 1 Thessalonians 5:17.

I once heard a man say that he prays when he awakes, before a
meal, and as he goes to bed. For him, this is what it means to constantly
pray.

On the other hand, I have a friend who prays when he sees the red-
and-blue-neon "Open" signs in storefront windows. He sees these signs
so often that it causes him to pray without ceasing.

How do you live out the command to "pray continually"?

*Walk and talk and work and laugh with your friends but
behind the scenes, keep up the life of simple prayer and inward
worship. Keep it up throughout the day.*[2]

—THOMAS KELLY

MODEL PRAYER

"This . . . is how you should pray:

'Our Father in heaven,
hallowed be your name,
your kingdom come,
your will be done
    on earth as it is in heaven.
Give us today our daily bread.
Forgive us our debts,
    as we also have forgiven our debtors.
And lead us not into temptation,
but deliver us from the evil one.'" (Matthew 6:9-13)

Jesus was teaching about prayer in Matthew 6:5-15. Read that passage for context.

This is the Lord's Prayer—the greatest prayer ever written. It is the prayer Jesus gave to His disciples when they asked Him how they should pray. It is a common prayer in the world, used by the saved and the unsaved alike.

Following are the components of this prayer. Rewrite each in your own words, drawing from your experiences and environment.

Adoration: "Our Father in heaven, hallowed be your name." Start by praising God for who He is.

Rule: "Your kingdom come, your will be done on earth as it is in heaven." Invite God to make an impact in your life and the world.

Bread: "Give us today our daily bread." Ask God to provide for your needs today.

Relationships: "Forgive us our debts, as we also have forgiven our debtors." Ask God to forgive your sins against Him and against humanity, and invite Him to show you where you have hurt others.

Strength: "And lead us not into temptation, but deliver us from the evil one." Invite God to speak to you about where you are weak and need to trust Him more.

Put the components together, and you will have your own version of the Lord's Prayer. Write your version below, and pray it to God.

None of us will keep up a life of prayer unless we are prepared to change. We will either give it up or turn it into a little system that maintains the form of godliness but denies the power of it—which is the same thing as giving it up. [3]

—RICHARD J. FOSTER

CHAPTER SIXTEEN

PURITY

What does it mean to live a pure life? There are various standards based on your age, the place where you live, and the commitments you have made. You are going to look at what the Bible has to say about living a pure life.

Purity is important in the follower of Christ for a few reasons. First, it is attempting to live a Christlike life. While you will not be able to live a sinless life, you should look toward Jesus' earthly life as your example. His life was pure.

Purity is also important because people will be looking to you as a follower of Christ for an example. They will judge the reality of God in your life by your actions.

Finally, you should work to live a pure life because it is the best for you. The pure life is easier than the complexities that arise in a corrupt life.

> *Before we can conquer the world, we must first conquer the self.* [1]

—J. OSWALD SANDERS

Memorize this and you will grow in your understanding of purity:

- Psalm 51:10
- Philippians 4:8

- Romans 6:13
- Proverbs 4:23

A MATTER OF THE HEART

Create in me a pure heart, O God,
and renew a steadfast spirit within me. (Psalm 51:10)

Read Psalm 51, and then pray it to God.

What is "a pure heart"? Put that concept into your own words.

If God is the one who creates a new heart within us, what is our responsibility?

What can you do to be steadfast for God?

THINGS TO THINK ABOUT

Brothers, whatever is true, whatever is noble, whatever is right, whatever is pure, whatever is lovely, whatever is admirable — if anything is excellent or praiseworthy — think about such things. (Philippians 4:8)

Paul was encouraging the church in Philippians 4:2-9. Read it for context.

We develop purity by thinking about things that are true, noble, right, pure, lovely, admirable, excellent, and praiseworthy. Let's put some names, faces, and places to these concepts.

What can you focus on that is true?

What can you focus on that is noble?

What can you focus on that is right?

What can you focus on that is pure?

What can you focus on that is lovely?

What can you focus on that is admirable?

What can you focus on that is excellent?

What can you focus on that is praiseworthy?

Now, what does it mean for you to focus on these things?

BODY OFFERING

Do not offer the parts of your body to sin, as instruments of wickedness, but rather offer yourselves to God, as those who have been brought from death to life; and offer the parts of your body to him as instruments of righteousness. (Romans 6:13)

For context, read Romans 6:1-14.

In Romans 6:13 there are two options for what you could offer your body to. What are they?

1.

2.

Your body can serve as an instrument for two very different purposes. It can be an instrument of _____ or an instrument of _____.

What does it mean for our bodies to be "instruments of wickedness"? What has that meant in your life?

What does it mean for them to be "instruments of righteousness"? How has your body been an instrument of righteousness?

If we offer our bodies to sin as instruments of wickedness, we are returning to _____.

If we offer our bodies to God as instruments of righteousness, we are not dead, but _____.

HEARTGUARD, LIFEGUARD

> Above all else, guard your heart,
>> for it is the wellspring of life. (Proverbs 4:23)

Read Proverbs 4.

There are many priorities in life. According to Proverbs 4:23, purity is to be number _____.

The heart was seen by the people of the biblical era as the center of one's personality. What does "heart" mean to you?

How might your heart be the "wellspring of life" for you?

Read 2 Kings 10:28-33.

What did Jehu do that pleased the Lord? (verses 28 and 30)

What did Jehu fail to do that he should have done? (verses 29 and 31)

What was the outcome of Jehu's actions? (verses 32-33)

What does this story teach you about the importance of guarding your heart?

CHAPTER SEVENTEEN

GIVING

As a maturing follower of Christ, you should grow in your understanding and practice of giving. Giving can be one of the most complicated and controversial issues you will face during your journey with Christ.

Giving is not just a donation of money, though that is what is often talked about. Giving is also a sharing of your time, possessions, and energy. There is much that we can give.

It is critical that you begin to ask Christ what He would have you give. Memorize this and it will prepare you for a lifetime of giving:

- Acts 4:32
- James 2:15-16
- 1 Peter 4:10
- Luke 12:15

ALL ONE

All the believers were one in heart and mind. No one claimed that any of his possessions was his own, but they shared everything they had. (Acts 4:32)

Read Acts 4:32-37.

What is the title for this section of the Bible? (If your Bible does not have titles, give this passage a title.)

What would it mean if all believers today were "one in heart and mind"?

Have you ever been part of a group—maybe a team, small group, church, or family—that was "one in heart and mind"? What was that experience like?

What would it look like if you didn't claim any of your possessions and shared everything with others?

What do you think would happen to your stuff?

How would you experience God differently if Acts 4:32 were true in your life?

The most creative social strategy we have to offer is the church. Here we show the world a manner of life the world can never achieve through social coercion or governmental action. We serve the world by showing it something that it is not, namely, a place where God is forming family out of strangers.[1]

—STANLEY HAUERWAS AND WILLIAM H. WILLIMON

BROTHER'S KEEPER

> Suppose a brother or sister is without clothes and daily
> food. If one of you says to him, "Go, I wish you well;
> keep warm and well fed," but does nothing about his
> physical needs, what good is it? (James 2:15-16)

James was writing about faith and deeds in James 2:14-26. Read it
for context.

In James 2:15-16, who is meant by "a brother or sister"?

This passage refers specifically to "clothes and daily food." But
what other "physical needs" are there that Christians ought to be
concerned about?

In Matthew 25:31-46, Jesus told the story of the sheep and the
goats. Read that story.

Which group looked after the physical needs of others—the
sheep or the goats?

What happened to the sheep?

What happened to the goats?

What can you learn from this story?

Answer the question of James 2:16: "If one of you says to him, 'Go, I wish you well; keep warm and well fed,' but does nothing about his physical needs, what good is it?"

GIFT GIVING

> Each one should use whatever gift he has received to serve others, faithfully administering God's grace in its various forms. (1 Peter 4:10)

Read Peter's teaching on living for God in 1 Peter 4:1-11.

What is meant by the word "gift" in 1 Peter 4:10?

Romans 12:6-8 lists some of the gifts God gives to His children. Read those verses.

What gifts or talents do you possess?

What does it mean to administer God's grace?

Read 1 Corinthians 4:2. What does this verse tell you about the use of your gifts?

Circle one of the gifts that you listed. How can you administer God's grace through the use of that gift this week?

MATERIALISM EXPOSED

"Watch out! Be on your guard against all kinds of greed; a man's life does not consist in the abundance of his possessions." (Luke 12:15)

Read Luke 12:13-21.

This interaction began with a man making a request of Jesus. What was the man asking for?

Jesus gave a two-point answer. What are the two points? (See verse 14 for the first point and verse 15 for the second point.)

1.

2.

Is there something you would love to have (maybe a game system, stereo, or car)? If so, identify it.

How will you remember that life does not consist of possessions?

What will happen to "anyone who stores up things for himself but is not rich toward God"? (verse 21)

CHAPTER EIGHTEEN

HUMILITY

Humility is a natural gift to some and a talent other people need to learn. Whatever it is for you, it is critical that as a follower of Christ you are humble.

In the same way that we cannot bring about our own salvation, there is nothing we have or are that comes from us. God alone provides all we have. Therefore, we don't take credit but humbly point to Him as the source and inspiration for our lives.

Memorize this and you will grow in humility:

- 1 Peter 3:8
- Jeremiah 9:23
- Ephesians 4:2
- James 3:13

HUMILITY AND THE CHRISTIAN VIRTUES

All of you, live in harmony with one another; be sympathetic, love as brothers, be compassionate and humble. (1 Peter 3:8)

Read 1 Peter 3:8-22.

The memory verse outlines a number of virtues that can enhance our faith journey with Christ. Let's break these down.

Read Romans 15:5-6. How do these verses enhance your understanding of what it means to "live in harmony with one another"? How have you experienced harmony with other Christians?

What does it mean to "be sympathetic"? Give an example from your life.

Read Romans 12:10. What do you learn about loving as brothers and sisters from this verse? How have you done this?

What does it mean to "be compassionate"? When have you been compassionate?

Define *humble* in your own words. Again, give an example of a time when you demonstrated that virtue in your life.

Read Proverbs 3:34. What do you receive from God if you are humble?

BACKING OFF FROM BOASTING

This is what the LORD says:

> "Let not the wise man boast of his wisdom
>   or the strong man boast of his strength
>   or the rich man boast of his riches." (Jeremiah 9:23)

Read Jeremiah 9.

In our day, what does it mean to be wise?

Most people would not walk around saying, "I'm smart," but they might boast of their wisdom in other ways. Give some examples of how they might do this.

How have you seen people (maybe your friends or classmates) boast of their strength?

Again, people probably wouldn't boast about their riches by telling people outright that they are rich. How might someone boast of his or her riches more subtly?

I'm sure you're smart, but maybe you don't have strength or riches. What do you boast of? Rewrite this verse with examples from your life.

Now Mama said there's only so much fortune a man really needs and the rest is just for showing off.

—FORREST GUMP IN *FORREST GUMP*

HUMILITY AND UNITY

Be completely humble and gentle; be patient, bearing with one another in love. (Ephesians 4:2)

Read Ephesians 4:1-16.

How many times are the words "one" or "unity" used in verses 1-6?

The first verse encourages us "to live a life worthy of the calling [we] have received." What does this mean?

The third verse encourages us "to keep the unity of the Spirit." How do we keep unity?

There are a number of "ones" mentioned in verses 4-6. List them.

What is the message of those verses?

The foundation of this passage is the memory verse. What can you learn about unity considering that this verse is the foundation?

THE WISDOM OF HUMILITY

Who is wise and understanding among you? Let him show it by his good life, by deeds done in the humility that comes from wisdom. (James 3:13)

Read James 3:13-18.

Start by answering the opening question: "Who is wise and understanding among you?" Write down the name of the wisest person you know.

What qualities make that person "wise and understanding," in your opinion?

Have you ever been a hero for someone else? Describe the situation.

When you acted heroically, how did you feel?

Describe how you demonstrated, or could have demonstrated, humility in that moment.

In this section of James, there are almost as many mentions of wisdom as there are of humility. What is the connection between wisdom and humility?

> It is better to have a small portion of wisdom with humility, and a slender understanding, than great treasures of sciences with vain self-esteem.[1]
>
> —THOMAS À KEMPIS

CHAPTER NINETEEN

PERSEVERANCE

As has been said before, your life journey with Christ will be a long journey. There will be challenges. There will be times when you feel alone. There will be growth pains. In the midst of all that, it is critical that you persevere.

Perseverance is not a popular word. Rather than persevere, we'd prefer to switch to an easy road. We go along with the idea that "if it's tough, it's not worth doing."

God, however, has a different way. His thinking is much more along the line of the old sports adage, "No pain, no gain." God asks us to persevere through the tough times, and by doing so, we grow into more complete followers of Jesus.

Memorize this and you will grow in your ability to persevere:

- James 1:12
- 2 Timothy 2:3
- Hebrews 6:11-12
- 1 Corinthians 4:2

A CROWN FOR ENDURANCE

Blessed is the man who perseveres under trial, because when he has stood the test, he will receive the crown of life that God has promised to those who love him. (James 1:12)

You read all of James 1 in chapter 14. Read James 1:1-18 as a refresher.

Have you ever faced a trial (maybe friends at school were making fun of your faith)? Describe the situation. How did you feel during that time?

How did God enhance your faith through that experience?

Did you feel blessed? Explain.

Look up the following verses. What do you learn about trials?

- James 1:2-3:

- 1 Peter 3:14:

SOLDIERING ON

Endure hardship with us like a good soldier of Christ Jesus. (2 Timothy 2:3)

Read 2 Timothy 2:1-13.

In his opening, the author encourages us to be strong in what?

What does it mean to "be strong in the grace that is in Christ Jesus"? (verse 1)

Why should we be strong in Christ and not in other things?

Does 2 Timothy 2:3 say, "*If* you have hardship, endure it"? Is enduring hardship an option, or does everyone go through it?

The author used two analogies: the soldier and the athlete. How do these two comparisons help you understand the need to endure hardship?

Why do we endure hardship? (verse 10)

TO THE VERY END

> We want each of you to show this same diligence to the very end, in order to make your hope sure. We do not want you to become lazy, but to imitate those who through faith and patience inherit what has been promised. (Hebrews 6:11-12)

Read the warning against falling away in Hebrews 5:11–6:12.

According to the memory verse, who should show diligence?

How long should we be diligent?

What is our hope?

How do we make our hope sure?

Have you ever been lazy (maybe you were sick or it was a rainy Sunday afternoon)? What did you do?

Who are we to imitate?

Define *faith* in your own words.

What do you learn about faith and patience from these verses?

- 2 Thessalonians 1:4-5:

- Hebrews 10:36:

- 1 Peter 1:6-7:

- Revelation 13:10:

Can you name a person who fits the positive description given in the memory verse?

How can you imitate that person on your faith journey?

> *The key to leadership development lies not in the experiences, whether good or bad, but in peoples' responses to those experiences.* [1]
>
> —HENRY AND RICHARD BLACKABY

LIVING UP TO A TRUST

It is required that those who have been given a trust must prove faithful. (1 Corinthians 4:2)

For context, read 1 Corinthians 4.

Who is the "us" that the author was referring to in verse 1?

Have you been given a "trust"? If so, what is it?

Who should "prove faithful"?

What must you do to be faithful with the trust God has given you? Be specific.

CHAPTER TWENTY

STUDY

Study is nothing new for you. You've been in school for years. Your parents and teachers have required you to study. Do you know that God requires you to study too?

God requires you to study His Word and also to be diligent in completing your studies at school. Study is important to God, it was important to Jesus during His time on earth, and it therefore should be important to us as well.

> *It soon becomes obvious that study demands humility. Study simply cannot happen until we are willing to be subject to the subject matter.*[1]
>
> —RICHARD J. FOSTER

Memorize this and you will be more dedicated to study:

- 1 Corinthians 14:20
- Psalm 119:34
- Proverbs 9:10
- Deuteronomy 4:9

GROWN-UP THOUGHTS

Brothers, stop thinking like children. In regard to evil be infants, but in your thinking be adults. (1 Corinthians 14:20)

Read 1 Corinthians 14.

When you were a child, what did you think about?

Did you have a favorite game you could play for hours or a television show you just had to see every week? Name it.

What does it mean to "stop thinking like children"?

What does it mean to "be infants" in regard to evil?

How does our thinking change as we grow up?

Why must we be like adults in our thinking?

How can you be more like an adult in your thinking?

Only a child gets prayer answered; a wise man does not.[2]

—OSWALD CHAMBERS

KNOWING AND OBEYING

> Give me understanding, and I will keep your law
>   and obey it with all my heart. (Psalm 119:34)

Read Psalm 119.

This psalm uses the word "understanding" in four ways. In each of the verses listed below, what are we to understand?

- Verse 27:

- Verse 73:

- Verse 144:

- Verse 169:

What can you conclude from these four verses about what God wants you to understand?

Psalm 119 is organized around the Hebrew alphabet. At the head of each section of the psalm (in many Bible versions), you will see a Hebrew letter introducing that section of this very long psalm.

Go through the psalm and, using the Hebrew letter from each section, think of something that God would like you to understand. For example, Aleph may be "the Almighty" and Heth might be "honor." Ask God to direct this exercise and give you insights into His will for your life.

THE BEGINNING OF WISDOM

The fear of the LORD is the beginning of wisdom,
and knowledge of the Holy One is understanding.
(Proverbs 9:10)

Read Proverbs 9.

What does it mean to fear the Lord?

How can fearing the Lord lead to wisdom?

Why is the term "Holy One" used to describe God?

How can you have knowledge of the Holy One?

Why are the terms "fear," "wisdom," "knowledge," and "understanding" used together in this verse?

What does that teach you about study?

RETENTION

> Only be careful, and watch yourselves closely so that you do not forget the things your eyes have seen or let them slip from your heart as long as you live. Teach them to your children and to their children after them.
> (Deuteronomy 4:9)

Read Deuteronomy 4:1-14.

Do you learn best by reading about a subject or by actually seeing it in action? Why?

Name one thing you have seen God do in your life, your church, your small group, or your family that you do not want to forget.

Why was that experience significant to you?

How can you make sure you don't forget that experience?

Why is it important to teach God's laws and share the ways He has worked in your life with your future children (if any)?

Ask your parents or older people in your church for stories about the ways God has acted on their behalf or on behalf of your faith community. Write down some of those experiences.

CHAPTER TWENTY-ONE

WORSHIP

For many people today, worship has become a narrowly defined concept meaning singing. But in God's vocabulary, worship is much larger. Worship is something we ought to be doing all the time, whether in a church service or while walking down the street.

To have a proper view of worship is to have a proper view of God. As you grow in your understanding of worship, you will also grow in your faith journey with Jesus.

> *Neither Bible nor church uses the word "worship" as a description of experience. Worship is neither subjective only nor private only. It is not what I feel when I am by myself; it is how I act toward God in responsible relation with God's people. Worship, in the biblical sources and in liturgical history, is not something a person experiences, it is something we do, regardless of how we feel about it.* [1]

—EUGENE PETERSON

Memorize this and you will worship:

- Psalm 95:6-7
- John 4:24
- Hebrews 13:15
- Ephesians 1:5-6

SHEPHERD PRAISE

> Come, let us bow down in worship,
>   let us kneel before the LORD our Maker;
> for he is our God
>   and we are the people of his pasture,
>   the flock under his care. (Psalm 95:6-7)

Read Psalm 95. Then go through the psalm in spirit, praying it to the Lord.

What does it mean to "sing for joy to the LORD"? (verse 1)

When have you been so happy or satisfied that you have sung to the Lord?

The second verse of the psalm encourages us to thank the Lord for what He has done. List some things God has done for you.

We can have many different priorities in life. Have you put any of your priorities ahead of God?

How can you express verses 4 and 5 in a prayer? What is God asking you to recognize?

When was the last time you bowed in worship or knelt in prayer?

Why don't you bow or kneel more often?

How has God cared for you? (verse 7) Write the ways.

Is your heart soft for God, or is it hard? (verse 8)

What can you do to soften your heart in worship?

SPIRITUAL WORSHIP

"God is spirit, and his worshipers must worship in spirit and in truth." (John 4:24)

Read about Jesus' interaction with a Samaritan woman in John 4:1-26.

What does it mean that "God is spirit"?

Who are His worshipers?

What does it mean to worship in spirit?

What does it mean to worship in truth?

Why are the words "spirit" and "truth" used together in this verse?

SACRIFICE OF PRAISE

Through Jesus . . . let us continually offer to God a sacrifice of praise—the fruit of lips that confess his name. (Hebrews 13:15)

Read Hebrews 13.

Our church had a youth choir called Adriel. Adriel had its big days when we were touring the country with two buses and an equipment truck, singing at churches and putting on great shows. The group was huge, and so were our performances.

Adriel also had its not-so-great days when Billy and I were the only tenors and we had to count on Chelle and Cindy to carry the tune for the girls. We didn't tour, and while we received a smattering of applause from our own congregation, I think they could have taken us or not.

When Adriel was large, we were excited about performing. But during the years that our choir was small, we just wanted to hide.

The good news is that regardless of the size or ability of Adriel, God accepted our "sacrifice of praise." Our praise was enough for Him.

What benefit comes from offering our praise through Jesus?

What does it mean to continually offer praise? How do you accomplish that?

What is the "fruit of [our] lips"?

Have there ever been times when "rotten fruit" has rolled off your lips? Describe it.

What changes can you make to ensure that you will continually confess the name of Jesus with your lips?

ADOPTED INTO GOD'S FAMILY

> He predestined us to be adopted as his sons through Jesus
> Christ, in accordance with his pleasure and will—to the
> praise of his glorious grace, which he has freely given us in
> the One he loves. (Ephesians 1:5-6)

Near the beginning of this study, you read the entire first chapter of
Ephesians. Reread the beautiful and powerful section of Ephesians 1:3-14.

What does "predestined" mean?

How are we adopted as God's children?

Why are we adopted?

How should the fact that we are adopted change the way we worship
God?

At this point you have finished the Life Issues stage of *Memorize This*.
It has asked you to consider some important concerns and required you
to memorize a number of additional verses, but you have done it all.
Good for you! Don't you feel more capable of handling whatever life
may send you—and doing it in a godly way? Give thanks to God and
enjoy the sense of accomplishment.

And now, there is one more stage to go in *Memorize This*.

LEADERSHIP

Today there are more books on leadership than there are leaders. Everyone is talking about the characteristics that make a leader and how to be a better one.

At this point in your faith journey, you are a leader. Either those above you have deemed you a leader, or you are a leader simply because of your age. Whatever the reason, it is critical that you understand your leadership role within your faith community.

As a young leader, one of your most important roles is witnessing. The word *witnessing* may bring to mind handing out Bible tracts, sharing your faith on street corners, or taking a bus full of kids to a rally. But while it may include those things, we are primarily talking about something different.

You are a witness to those around you all the time. How you live your life, the way you show love, the method in which you use the Word, the manner in which you seek out justice—all of these actions are opportunities to witness to those you influence (which at this point in your faith journey is probably more people than you realize). Witnessing is all-encompassing.

For example, you invite a kid to go shopping with you. How do you treat the salesperson? This is witnessing with your life. On the way home, the student asks you, "Why should I go to the Sunday morning worship?" You give an answer that includes one of the verses you memorized earlier in this book. This is witnessing with the Word.

You are a leader whether you see it or not. Live what you are and take on that leadership role. Don't wear it like a military uniform but instead as a servant's cloak. Serve those around you by being a witness.

CHAPTER TWENTY-TWO

WITNESS BY LOVE

Love is an interesting word that can mean many different things. You can love your girlfriend or boyfriend and you can love your car, but *love* means very different things in those two situations (I hope!).

In the original Bible languages, there were many different words that meant *love*. Today, with only one word to express the various meanings, we need to look closely at this concept and grow in our understanding of what it means to love.

Love is the greatest language. It can communicate vast ideas, as shown in the Bible: "All men will know that you are my disciples, if you love one another" (John 13:35).

Memorize this and you will be a greater witness by love:

- 1 Thessalonians 3:12
- John 15:12
- Luke 6:27-28
- 1 Corinthians 13:4-5
- 1 Peter 4:8
- Matthew 5:44

LOVE OVERFLOWING

May the Lord make your love increase and overflow for each other and for everyone else, just as ours does for you. (1 Thessalonians 3:12)

Read 1 Thessalonians 3:6-13.

When I was part of the leadership team for a youth club, we had one student, Erik, who came to every event we held. If it was Monday night, our usual club night, we could expect to see Erik in the crowd. If we were going to camp, he would be the first with a deposit.

In addition, you couldn't miss Erik. He was full of energy and fun at every event, always causing some kind of mischief. We loved this guy!

Yet despite the fact that he came to every major event we held, he had not committed his life to Christ. He had the information and had heard the invitation, but though many of Erik's classmates stood up to indicate faith in Christ, he did not. We put on excellent events with all the extras—almost as if they were designed for Erik, who was so committed to us but not to Christ—but nothing took.

One time during his senior year, Erik needed a ride home following one of our weekly meetings. Our leadership team met after the club meeting, so I told him that he could have a ride but that he'd have to come with me to the leadership meeting first.

During the leadership meeting, we prayed, laughed, and planned as a team. Meanwhile, this usually energetic kid sat quietly and watched.

After the meeting, I drove Erik home. Again he sat quietly—not his usual mode of operation. When we arrived at his house, he didn't get out of the car. After a minute of silence, he spoke: "I've never been around a group that loved each other so much. I want to be a part of that kind of group."

That was the night Erik committed his life to Christ. It wasn't after one of our show-stopping weekly meetings. It wasn't after a trip to one of our first-class camps. It wasn't after all his friends had committed themselves to the Lord. It was after he saw a group of people love each other as Christ loves us.

Witnessing by love changed Erik's life.

Who is the Erik in your life—someone to whom you can witness by love? (Note: It would be ideal to choose someone of the same gender.)

How can you show him or her love? That is, how can you "overflow" with love?

> *Do we want to help people because we feel sorry for them, or because we genuinely love them? The world needs something deeper than pity; it needs love. (How trite that sounds, how real it is!)*[1]

—THOMAS KELLY

LOVING LIKE JESUS

"My command is this: Love each other as I have loved you." (John 15:12)

You've read part of John 15 before, but for context, read John 15:1-17.

If your Bible has section titles, write the title for this section. Create one if it does not.

Who is speaking in this section? (If you have a Bible with red print, this should be easy.)

How did Jesus show His love to us?

In the memory verse we are asked to love others the way Jesus loved us. How can we do that?

Jesus didn't say, "I strongly suggest . . . " or "If you want to . . . " or "When you feel all right. . . ." Instead, this verse is a command. We *must* love each other.

UNEXPECTED RESPONSE

"I tell you who hear me: Love your enemies, do good to those who hate you, bless those who curse you, pray for those who mistreat you." (Luke 6:27-28)

This is not a command I find easy to follow. I want to hate my enemies. I want to hate those who hate me. I want to curse those who curse me. I want to mistreat those who mistreat me. That is the feeling I have in my gut.

But Jesus turned it all around—I'm not supposed to act with my gut. There is a new command to love. This is radical teaching.

Read Luke 6:27-36.

Who was Jesus talking to in this account?

If you get tripped on the way to class, what are your classmates going to expect you to do?

How can you react in a Christlike way instead?

Some people will have negative comments about your Christlike reaction, but others will have positive comments. Write down some of the positive comments people might make.

We can witness to our faith in Jesus by returning hateful actions with love.

SUCH IS LOVE

> Love is patient, love is kind. It does not envy, it does not boast, it is not proud. It is not rude, it is not self-seeking, it is not easily angered, it keeps no record of wrongs.
> (1 Corinthians 13:4-5)

First Corinthians 13 is probably the most popular passage on love in the Bible. Certainly it is the most commonly used Bible passage for weddings. Read all of 1 Corinthians 13.

From verses 4-7, what are the eight things that love *is*?

From the same section, what are the seven characteristics that love *is not*?

Many people in our society are not patient. How can you love people by being patient?

It is easy to boast and be proud of what we do. We are asked here not to be boastful, proud, or self-seeking when we love other people. How do you practice humility in loving someone?

Are you keeping a record of wrongs against somebody? Have you become easily angered with someone? If so, how can you correct both of those situations?

Has someone ever loved you as expressed in this chapter? Describe what that experience was like and how it impacted your life.

LOVE'S DEEP WELL

Above all, love each other deeply, because love covers over a multitude of sins. (1 Peter 4:8)

You've read it before, but read 1 Peter 4:1-11 again as a refresher.

Love in action is expressed in verses 9-11:

- "Offer _____ to one another without grumbling." (verse 9)
- Use your gifts to _____ others. (verse 10)
- Speak the very words of _____. (verse 11)
- Serve with the _____ of God. (verse 11)

What do these verses together teach you about love?

We love to care for people because of the effect it has on them, but loving others does something for us as well. How have you benefited from loving, caring for, or helping somebody?

LOVE FOR ENEMIES

"I tell you: Love your enemies and pray for those who persecute you." (Matthew 5:44)

Jesus was teaching about loving our enemies in Matthew 5:43-48. Read this passage.

Matthew 5:44 is part of what famous teaching of Jesus? You'll have to look at the broader context for the answer.

As a little kid, was there somebody you really didn't like?
(Thinking of yourself as Spiderman, who was your Green
Goblin—your archenemy?)

Why was this person your enemy?

Do you have someone in school or at work today with whom you
struggle to relate? If so, write that person's name.

In the memory verse, Jesus gives you two things to do for that person.
What are they?

How can you love that person this week?

Develop a plan to pray for that person this week. Write it down.

CHAPTER TWENTY-THREE

WITNESS BY LIFE

St. Francis of Assisi said, "Preach the gospel. When necessary, use words."

There are hundreds of ways to be a witness for Christ without using words.

Witnessing is not simply an activity; it is a way of life.

Followers of Christ should have discernible differences from the rest of the world. A great example of this is the owner of the Chick-Fil-A restaurant chain. When people go past a Chick-Fil-A restaurant on a Sunday and see it closed among the many restaurants that are open, they must ask, "Why?" The answer is that this restaurant is closed on Sundays because of the owner's spiritual convictions. This is a discernible difference, and few people miss it.

Discernible differences are those things that set followers of Christ apart from the rest of the world. This is a form of witness, especially when it is done humbly and with the right motivation.

Memorize this and your life will provide a better witness:

- Luke 22:26
- Ephesians 5:17
- 1 Corinthians 8:9
- 2 Timothy 2:2
- 1 Peter 1:15-16
- Galatians 5:22-23

SERVANT LEADERSHIP

"You are not to be like that. Instead, the greatest among you should be like the youngest, and the one who rules like the one who serves." (Luke 22:26)

Read Luke 22:7-38.

Where was Jesus when He said this?

Who was He talking to?

What was about to happen to Jesus?

It is especially important for you to have the context of this verse, as it is part of a longer conversation. Jesus told His followers that they were "not to be like that." Like what?

Jesus said, "The greatest among you should be like the youngest, and the one who rules like the one who serves." What did Jesus do early in the dinner party to model this behavior?

Are you the youngest sibling in your family? If so, what is that like? (If you are not the youngest, ask a younger brother or sister what it is like.)

Spend a night serving your family. Make them dinner, serve it to them, clean up afterward, and offer them dessert. Following that exercise, write about the experience.

How was serving your family a witness to them?

LIVING GOD'S WILL

> Do not be foolish, but understand what the Lord's will is.
> (Ephesians 5:17)

Part of having a life that is a witness is avoiding foolishness and walking as the Lord would have you walk. Read Ephesians 5:15-21.

In these verses, Paul (the author) gave us seven principles for living life.

1. "Be very _____." (verse 15)
2. Make the most of _____ opportunity. (verse 16)
3. Follow the Lord. (verse 17)
4. "Be filled with the _____." (verse 18)
5. Praise the Lord. (verse 19)
6. Always be giving _____. (verse 20)
7. "_____ to one another." (verse 21)

Let's apply these seven principles to your life.

In your walk with Christ, how should you be careful? What are the places or people you have to be careful around?

Life offers many opportunities. What does it mean to make the most of every one?

To avoid being foolish and to follow the will of the Lord means to be discerning. How do you discern the Lord's will for your life?

Wine is one of many kinds of spirits (another name for alcohol). Verse 18 tells you not to be filled with that spirit but to be filled instead with the Spirit of God. How do you know you are filled with His Spirit?

Be grateful. What are you thankful for today?

Few people like to submit, but verse 21 tells us that we should submit to each other. Is that difficult for you? If so, why?

Follow these seven principles and your life will not be a foolish witness.

FREEDOM IN CHECK

> Be careful . . . that the exercise of your freedom does not
> become a stumbling block to the weak. (1 Corinthians 8:9)

Read 1 Corinthians 8 for context.

Imagine you are with a group of your church friends, laughing
and joking. It's all innocent at first, but then you start talking negatively about a school acquaintance (an unbeliever). Just as the
juiciest part of the gossip is pouring from your lips, the person
you are talking about walks up behind you and overhears. What
do you think this person's impression of you will be?

What will this person think about followers of Christ?

What will the chances be that this person will commit to following Christ?

We have been given great freedom in Christ and a wonderful
fellowship with other followers. But we can become careless with
our actions and words, thereby hurting others. So let's be cautious.
We want to have a positive life witness, not a negative one.

THE MULTIPLICATION PRINCIPLE

> The things you have heard me say in the presence of many witnesses entrust to reliable men who will also be qualified to teach others. (2 Timothy 2:2)

Second Timothy is a short book. You've read part of it before, but this time read the entire book in one sitting.

A shampoo commercial on television started with a woman saying her shampoo was so good that she told two friends about it. The screen then split, and the two friends said they were so impressed with the shampoo that they told two friends about it. The screen split again, and all four people said they were so impressed that they told two friends. The commercial continued until the screen was full of little heads saying, "And so on, and so on, and so on. . . ."

We have something great to share as well—much more important than any shampoo! And if we witness with our lives to the right people, the message will spread first to them and then from them to others. And so on, and so on, and so on. . . .

Second Timothy 2:2 presents this reality as four levels of sharing:

The first level was that of the author, the apostle Paul. He was the one who had spoken "in the presence of many witnesses."

The second level was that of the persons to whom Paul was writing "the things you have heard."

Who would constitute the third level of sharing? Men who were

_____ and also _____.

The final level was that of the people who would receive the message from the "reliable men."

Now apply the four levels to your life in the following questions:

The first level is made up of the people from whom you heard the message of Christ. Who helped initiate your life journey with Christ?

The second level is you.

The third level is composed of those to whom you are passing on what you have learned. Who are those people?

Are they reliable? How do you know?

Are they qualified to teach others? How do you know?

The fourth level is made up of those to whom the reliable, qualified people are passing on the message. Do you know any of these fourth-level people? If so, write down some of their names.

> *You must discipline yourself to . . . look on the various facets of your ministry as opportunities to build in depth into the lives of your potential workers. This will enable you to keep your priorities straight, and you will be able to gauge what you do by how it contributes to your prime*

objective of developing spiritually qualified workers. Your min-
istry will have meaning only as it contributes to the maturing of
these men. [1]

—LEROY EIMS

HOLY LIKE GOD

Just as he who called you is holy, so be holy in all you do; for
it is written: "Be holy, because I am holy." (1 Peter 1:15-16)

Read 1 Peter 1:13-25.

The author gave five commands in verses 13-15. What are they?

1.

2.

3.

4.

5.

The phrase "Be holy, because I am holy" comes from three passages in
Leviticus. Read those verses and the surrounding text. What additional
insights do you learn from each?

• Leviticus 11:44-45:

• Leviticus 19:2:

• Leviticus 20:7:

This section is titled "Be Holy" in many Bibles. Based on the five commands of Peter and the passages from Leviticus, what would you say it means to be holy?

How is your understanding of what it means to be holy going to change what you do tomorrow?

THE CHOICEST FRUIT

> The fruit of the Spirit is love, joy, peace, patience, kindness, goodness, faithfulness, gentleness and self-control. Against such things there is no law. (Galatians 5:22-23)

Read Galatians 5:16-26.

According to the author, there are two natures within each of us. Name them.

1.

2.

How have you seen the sinful nature evidenced in your life?

Galatians 5:22-23 lists the fruit of the Spirit. Which kinds of fruit do you have a basketful of?

Which do you need to shop for because they don't come easily to you?

In what ways have the fruit of the Spirit and your sinful nature battled? Give examples.

CHAPTER TWENTY-FOUR

WITNESS BY JUSTICE

When I was a kid, all the world's superheroes met in one place—
the Justice League. It didn't matter that they had different special
powers; they united under a common banner to rid the world of
injustice.

Our call as followers of Christ is not much different. We are
called to promote justice in the world. We will not have the same
special powers, but we do all have supernatural powers provided by
the Holy Spirit.

Followers of Christ are called to help the downtrodden, care
for the ill, and find the lost. This is the example set forth by Jesus.
We are called to fight for justice, not with a sword, but with love
and peace.

> *The gospels show Jesus taking particular notice of those
> who were on the underside of his society.*[1]
>
> —PETE WARD

Striving for justice is a popular objective today. Examples
include U2's Bono working for the depressed countries of the
world, the United States providing humanitarian relief to Third
World countries, and the International Justice Mission seeking out
justice for those forced to perform slave labor.

The cry for justice is the same throughout the world: "No justice, no peace." And the world is listening. Are you?

Memorize this and be a part of the real Justice League:

- Deuteronomy 27:19
- Psalm 106:3
- Proverbs 21:3
- Isaiah 1:17
- Jeremiah 9:24
- Zechariah 7:9

JUSTICE FOR THE NEEDY

Cursed is the man who withholds justice from the alien, the fatherless or the widow.
     Then all the people shall say,
               "Amen!" (Deuteronomy 27:19)

Read Deuteronomy 27.

Explain the context of this verse.

What does it mean to be "cursed"?

Define "alien," "fatherless," and "widow" in your own terms.

- Alien:

- Fatherless:

• Widow:

Now put names and faces to those three categories. Among the people you know, who fits these categories? (You can stretch each category a bit if you need to. For example, if you don't know an actual widow, write the name of a friend who recently went through a tough breakup with a boyfriend or girlfriend.)

• Alien:
• Fatherless:
• Widow:

DOING WHAT IS RIGHT

Blessed are they who maintain justice,
who constantly do what is right. (Psalm 106:3)

Read Psalm 106.

Think of somebody in your realm of influence who is not treated justly. It may be somebody who is made fun of or even somebody who is physically abused. How can you bring justice to that person?

In addition to bringing justice to a single situation, we also can work against systemic injustice (that is, injustice that exists in an entire system, such as an institution or government). For example, if a building does not allow for wheelchair access, those with disabilities face injustice by the owners of the building. Maintaining justice means correcting systemic injustice as well as individual injustice.

What is a systemic injustice in your realm of influence?

What can you do to bring justice to that situation?

This verse isn't just about bringing justice. The second half says that we need to constantly do what?

Never inflict injustice upon one person or group in order to give justice to another. For example, if a friend of yours was being picked on and you beat up the person who was picking on your friend, you would be trading one injustice for another. Be sure to "constantly do what is right."

THE VALUE OF JUSTICE

> To do what is right and just
>   is more acceptable to the LORD than sacrifice.
>   (Proverbs 21:3)

Read Proverbs 21 for context.

What is meant here by "sacrifice"?

What are some things you do just because they seem like the "Christian" thing to do?

In your mind, picture a high road and a low road. The low road represents those things that we do because "that's what we've always done" or "that's what the best Christians do." The high road represents what is truly right and just in the eyes of God.

What does it mean for you to take the high road?

LESSONS IN JUSTICE

"Learn to do right!
Seek justice,
    encourage the oppressed.
Defend the cause of the fatherless,
    plead the case of the widow." (Isaiah 1:17)

Read Isaiah 1.

Who is speaking in verse 17?

On whose behalf is he speaking? (See verse 20.)

God tells us to *learn* to do right. He doesn't expect us to naturally *know* how to do right. What can you do today to learn how to do right?

God takes us a step beyond *doing* justice and asks us to *seek* justice. How can you seek justice in your realm of influence?

Who are the oppressed in your community?

How can you encourage them without belittling them?

THE GREAT JUDGE

> "Let him who boasts boast about this:
>   that he understands and knows me,
> that I am the LORD, who exercises kindness,
>   justice and righteousness on earth,
>   for in these I delight,"
>   declares the LORD. (Jeremiah 9:24)

You've read Jeremiah 9 once before. Read it once again.

Statues stand in front of many old courthouses and in many courtrooms. They usually are of a blindfolded woman holding a sword and a scale. These statues are more than just artwork; the elements in them represent aspects of justice.

The woman is meant to represent chastity, a person who is virtuous and uncorrupted. She is blindfolded to show that her justice does not depend on the look of a person. The scale represents the manner in which evidence is to be weighed, that is, minutely. Finally, the sword is in her hand ready to strike when guilt is determined.

Our God is a God of justice. While there may be an inability to carry out justice in our system, God's justice is pure. He has the ability to see people beyond their clothes, skin, and appearance. In this way, He is kind. He is able to weigh evidence down to the smallest of details. By this, He is righteous. But God's justice is also to be greatly feared because He is able to carry out the stiffest and most lethal punishment.

We have the privilege of partnering in God's justice. We are His "statuettes" on the earth. We operate not out of our own power but out of His, bringing His justice to our communities.

Where is there injustice in your community?

God asks us to be humble. But if we are to boast, what are we to boast about?

Name the three things in which the LORD delights.

    1.
    2.
    3.

How are you bringing each to your community? Give specific examples.

    1.

2.

3.

JUSTICE AND MERCY

"This is what the LORD Almighty says: 'Administer true justice; show mercy and compassion to one another.'" (Zechariah 7:9)

Read Zechariah 7.

God says to "administer true justice." Could there be untrue justice? What would that look like? Can you give an example?

What does it mean for you to administer true justice?

Define *mercy* in your own words.

What does it mean for you to show mercy?

What does *compassion* mean?

What does it mean for you to show compassion?

Rewrite this verse, personalized for you: "This is what the LORD Almighty says. . . ."

CHAPTER TWENTY-FIVE

WITNESS BY WORD

We can witness by loving people, by our life or example, and even by bringing justice to the world, but at some point we are going to have to talk about our faith. This is witness by our words.

It is often important to build a bridge to our unbelieving friends as we begin to witness to them. We do this by loving them and being a Christlike example. Eventually though, we are going to have to cross that bridge and share with them the reason for our actions.

If we do not speak to our friends about Christ, we not only do them an eternal disservice, but we also leave our actions spiritually powerless.

Memorize this and you will be a better witness by word:

- Mark 16:15
- Luke 6:45
- 1 Corinthians 2:12-13
- Ephesians 6:19
- Proverbs 16:24
- 2 Timothy 2:15

A GREAT COMMISSION

He said to them, "Go into all the world and preach the good news to all creation." (Mark 16:15)

Read Mark 16.

Who is the audience for Jesus' statement in this verse?

What had just happened?

We immediately think of "all the world" in geographical terms. What could "all the world" mean from the angle of social status?

When we see the word "preach," we might think of a pastor standing behind a pulpit. Yet few of us are pastors who own our own portable pulpits. How else could you think of the word "preach"?

Finally, what is the "good news"?

AUTHENTIC MESSAGE

> "The good man brings good things out of the good stored up in his heart, and the evil man brings evil things out of the evil stored up in his heart. For out of the overflow of his heart his mouth speaks." (Luke 6:45)

Read Luke 6:43-45.

Give this section a title. (If your Bible gives section titles, use something different.)

Draw a picture of a tree. (You don't have to be an artist; just do your best.)

What good fruit is coming from your life? Write your "fruit" on the tree you drew.

All of us will have a few rotten apples on our tree. Write the bad fruit on your tree.

According to Luke 6:45, where does the good in your life come from?

Where does the evil come from?

Where do the words that come out of your mouth originate?

How can you make sure that there is more good in your heart and less evil?

SPIRITUAL WORDS

> We have not received the spirit of the world but the Spirit
> who is from God, that we may understand what God has
> freely given us. This is what we speak, not in words taught us
> by human wisdom but in words taught by the Spirit, express-
> ing spiritual truths in spiritual words. (1 Corinthians 2:12-13)

Read 1 Corinthians 2:6-16.

In this passage, how many times are words like "speak," "instruct,"
"teach," and "words" used?

Why the emphasis on words such as those?

Explain the term "spirit of the world." What does this mean? How
have you experienced this?

Who is "the Spirit who is from God"?

Why have we received this Spirit?

What do we teach?

Explain what you think the writer meant by "spiritual words."

BOLDNESS

Pray also for me, that whenever I open my mouth, words may be given me so that I will fearlessly make known the mystery of the gospel. (Ephesians 6:19)

Read Ephesians 6:10-20.

In this passage we are instructed to get ready for battle. Who is our fight against?

Draw a line between each piece of armor and its spiritual component.

Helmet	Truth
Breastplate	Faith
Belt	Spirit, Word of God
Shield	Salvation
Sword	Righteousness

The passage ends with two calls to pray. In verse 18, for whom are we called to pray?

Secondly, who are we called to pray for in verse 19?

SWEET AS HONEY

> Pleasant words are a honeycomb,
>> sweet to the soul and healing to the bones.
>> (Proverbs 16:24)

Read Proverbs 16.

What is your favorite sweet? A Krispy Kreme doughnut? A caramel macchiato from Starbucks? Ben & Jerry's Chunky Monkey ice cream? Name it.

Now rewrite the beginning of Proverbs 16:24: "Pleasant words are a _____ [insert your favorite sweet], sweet to the soul. . . ."

How can you tell when your soul has heard pleasant words?

What do you think "healing to the bones" means?

Now that we've analyzed the whole verse, put it back together in your own words.

A WORKER APPROVED

> Do your best to present yourself to God as one approved,
> a workman who does not need to be ashamed and who
> correctly handles the word of truth. (2 Timothy 2:15)

You've read 2 Timothy before. Gain context for this verse by reading 2 Timothy 2:14-19 again.

Drawing from the memory verse, what are two ways you can present yourself to God?

How can you make sure you are not ashamed when you go before God?

While the other verses in this section focus on the words from our mouth, this verse directly speaks to "the word of truth," the Bible. What does it mean to correctly handle Scripture?

How can you improve in your ability to use the Bible?

CONCLUSION

Memorize This has been an incredible journey for you. But you still have one short exercise to complete in the program. This exercise should be like a photo album that will help you recall the trip you've taken.

Think back over your progress through this book. Can you remember the day you started *Memorize This?* Describe yourself at that time. What did you look like? How did you feel about yourself? What was the condition of your relationship with God?

As you know, life with Christ is a journey full of excitement, adventure, and fun.

As you worked through this book, what were some exciting insights or conversations you had?

How was *Memorize This* an adventure for you?

Describe a situation during the course of this study that was fun—a time when you laughed and had a great time.

Any journey, including the journey of following Jesus, is also full of challenges, struggles, and difficulties.

I can remember the summer before my senior year when I traveled with my parents through Scandinavia. It was a great time, but three weeks into the trip, my dad and I had the biggest fight of our relationship. I thought we were going to come to blows! Journeys can be rough.

As you worked through *Memorize This*, what was your greatest challenge? Why?

Was there a time when you had a personal struggle (such as a time when you were inconsistent in your morality)? Describe that situation.

Finally, what was the most difficult verse for you to memorize? Why?

Memorize This was designed to assist you in each stage of your journey with Christ—to help you celebrate the excitement, adventure, and fun as well as carry you through the challenges, struggles, and difficulties of life. But don't stop now. Continue to use the Bible to guide your journey with Christ.

You have been given a tremendous resource. The Bible is one of the key tools that God has given you. Now that you know how to use it better, put it to use more in your life.

Build on the pattern you have developed to study and memorize Scripture by finding a new study or memorization program you can use. The *Topical Memory System* is a tool that has been used by followers of Christ for generations. There are many others as well.

Ask the mentors who supported you through *Memorize This* to help you develop a next step. They will know best—probably better than you—what you will need. Trust their insights. Ask for their help. At this point you may operate in more of a peer, rather than mentor, relationship.

No matter how you move, the point is to keep moving forward. The greatest challenge for the young follower of Christ is overcoming the temptation to stop, plateau, or put spiritual work to the side. If you don't move forward, all that you gained through this study will fade into distant memories. You don't want to waste what you've accomplished.

Memorization is not easy, especially in the midst of your busy life. Yet amid work, friends, sports, church, homework, and many other distractions, you have completed *Memorize This*.

This study has probably impacted every part of your life. You've most likely seen changes in your attitude, your relationships, and your journey with Christ. This should encourage you to grow all the more.

And God has been with you in this incredible journey. He has been cheering you on throughout, and now, as you cross the finish line of this marathon, He is there to celebrate with you. Congratulations!

NOTES

Introduction

1. J. Robert Clinton, *The Making of a Leader* (Colorado Springs, Colo.: NavPress, 1988), p. 89.
2. Thomas Kelly, *A Testament of Devotion* (New York: Harper & Brothers, 1941), p. 61.

Stage one: New Believer

1. Oswald Chambers, *My Utmost for His Highest* (Grand Rapids, Mich.: Discovery House, 1935), p. 88.

Chapter one: Assurance of God's Love

1. Henri J. M. Nouwen, *Life of the Beloved: Spiritual Living in a Secular World* (New York: Crossroad, 1992), p. 39.

Chapter two: Assurance of Jesus

1. *Design for Discipleship: Your Life in Christ* (Colorado Springs, Colo.: NavPress, 1973), p. 13.

Chapter three: Assurance of Forgiveness

1. Philip Yancey, *The Jesus I Never Knew* (New York: Walker, 1995), p. 82.

Chapter four: Assurance of Strength

1. Thomas à Kempis, *The Imitation of Christ* (Uhrichsville, Ohio: Barbour, 1984), Book 3, XXXVI, 3.

Chapter five: Assurance of an Answer

1. Richard J. Foster, *Prayer* (San Francisco: HarperSanFrancisco, 1992), p. 11.

Chapter six: Assurance of Eternal Life

1. Henri J. M. Nouwen, *The Wounded Healer: Ministry in Contemporary Society* (New York: Doubleday, 1972), p. 19.

Chapter seven: Assurance of Guidance

1. Pete Ward, *God at the Mall: Youth Ministry That Meets Kids Where They're At* (Peabody, Mass.: Hendrickson, 1999), p. 99.

Chapter eight: Disciple of God

1. Thomas à Kempis, *The Imitation of Christ* (Uhrichsville, Ohio: Barbour, 1984), Book 3, XLIII, 2.

Chapter nine: Disciple of Christ

1. Henri J. M. Nouwen, *The Wounded Healer: Ministry in Contemporary Society* (New York: Doubleday, 1972), p. 20.
2. J. Oswald Sanders, *Spiritual Leadership* (Chicago: Moody, 1994), p. 16.
3. Michael Yaconelli, *Dangerous Wonder: The Adventure of Childlike Faith* (Colorado Springs, Colo.: NavPress, 1998), p. 22.

Chapter eleven: Disciple of Others

1. J. Oswald Sanders, *Spiritual Leadership* (Chicago: Moody, 1994), p. 23.
2. Eugene Peterson, *Five Smooth Stones for Pastoral Work* (Grand Rapids, Mich.: Eerdmans, 1980), p. 209.
3. Thomas Kelly, *A Testament of Devotion* (New York: Harper & Brothers, 1941), p. 83.

Chapter thirteen: Disciple for Christ

1. Henri J. M. Nouwen, *Life of the Beloved: Spiritual Living in a Secular World* (New York: Crossroad, 1992), p. 85.

Chapter fourteen: Love

1. Henri J. M. Nouwen, *Life of the Beloved: Spiritual Living in a Secular World* (New York: Crossroad, 1992), pp. 53-54.
2. J. Oswald Sanders, *Spiritual Leadership* (Chicago: Moody, 1994), p. 75.
3. Henri J. M. Nouwen, *The Wounded Healer: Ministry in Contemporary Society* (New York: Doubleday, 1972), p. 72.

Chapter fifteen: Prayer

1. J. Oswald Sanders, *Spiritual Leadership* (Chicago: Moody, 1994), p. 87.
2. Thomas Kelly, *A Testament of Devotion* (New York: Harper & Brothers, 1941), p. 39.
3. Richard J. Foster, *Prayer* (San Francisco: HarperSanFrancisco, 1992), p. 57.

Chapter sixteen: Purity

1. J. Oswald Sanders, *Spiritual Leadership* (Chicago: Moody, 1994), p. 52.

Chapter seventeen: Giving

1. Stanley Hauerwas and William H. Willimon, *Resident Aliens: Life in the Christian Colony* (Nashville: Abingdon, 1989), p. 83.

Chapter eighteen: Humility

1. Thomas à Kempis, *The Imitation of Christ* (Uhrichsville, Ohio: Barbour, 1984), Book 3, VII, 3.

Chapter nineteen: Perseverance

1. Henry and Richard Blackaby, *Spiritual Leadership: Moving People on to God's Agenda* (Nashville: Broadman, Holman, 2001), p. 41.

Chapter twenty: Study

1. Richard J. Foster, *Celebration of Discipline: The Path to Spiritual Growth*, rev. ed. (San Francisco: Harper & Row, 1988), p. 66.
2. Oswald Chambers, *My Utmost for His Highest* (Grand Rapids, Mich.: Discovery House, 1935), p. 291.

Chapter twenty-one: Worship

1. Eugene Peterson, *Five Smooth Stones for Pastoral Work* (Grand Rapids, Mich.: Eerdmans, 1980), p. 183.

Chapter twenty-two: Witness by Love

1. Thomas Kelly, *A Testament of Devotion* (New York: Harper & Brothers, 1941), p. 123.

Chapter twenty-three: Witness by Life

1. LeRoy Eims, *The Lost Art of Disciple Making* (Colorado Springs, Colo.: NavPress, 1978), p. 104.

Chapter twenty-four: Witness by Justice

1. Pete Ward, *God at the Mall: Youth Ministry That Meets Kids Where They're At* (Peabody, Mass.: Hendrickson, 1999), p. 118.

ABOUT THE AUTHOR

D. MASON RUTLEDGE is the director of training for Young Life and a volunteer WyldLife leader. Furthermore, he is an adjunct professor at Western Seminary in Portland, Oregon, and Eastern University in St. David's, Pennsylvania. Mason serves on the executive council of the National Network of Youth Ministers and holds a master of divinity degree from Fuller Theological Seminary. He and his wife, Brenda, live in Colorado Springs, Colorado, with their three children, Merrick, Madison, and Murdock.

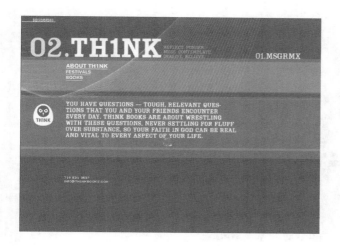

POP QUIZ

Why is th1nkbooks.com spelled with a one instead
of an I?
    a) it holds deep symbolic meaning
    b) www.thinkbooks.com was already taken
    c) the owl told us to do it

Check out upcoming releases from TH1NK BOOKS,
sign up for our street teams, and chat with other
readers . . . bookmark www.th1nkbooks.com.

No games, no masks—God accepts us as we are.

Posers, Fakers, & Wannabes
Unmasking the Real You
Brennan Manning and Jim Hancock
1-57683-465-4

God isn't fooled by the games we play, the masks we wear. And as much as we try, we'll never fake our way into his affection.

The best part is: the Father already knows and accepts us exactly as we are. He knows how we think and act; He knows our dreams and fears. Brennan and Jim explain how God's total acceptance of us sets us free to be who we really are.

Practice your faith. Every day.

Read, Think, Pray, Live
A guide to reading the Bible in a new way
Tony Jones
1-57683-453-0

If you want to know Jesus and what He's all about, try doing these four—read, think, pray, live. It's how your faith can grow. *Lectio divina*, or sacred reading, is a time-tested method used by believers to experience God in a personal and real way.

Tailored for students, this book teaches you how to engage your faith. Learning from a method of contemplative study that has worked for hundreds of years, you'll find yourself challenged and encouraged to get to know God in brand-new ways.

1-800-366-7788
www.th1nkbooks.com

THINK

Because they don't offer Talking to God 101.
(Even though they should.)

Pray
Tony Jones
1-57683-452-2

Do you ever feel a little stumped about prayer—like you keep saying the same things over and over again? Maybe you don't know how to get started.

With this book, you'll learn by the solid example of those who have gone before us. The prayers of these men and women—the prophets, the apostles, the early and modern church, and even Jesus himself—can help us pray more effectively. Author Tony Jones highlights the important features of these powerful prayers—so you can enjoy talking to God as much as they did.

The Message Remix
Eugene H. Peterson
Hardcover
1-57683-434-4
Bonded Alligator Leather
1-57683-450-6

God's Word was meant to be read and understood. It was first written in the language of the people—of fishermen, shopkeepers, and carpenters. *The Message Remix* gets back to that feel. Plus the new verse-numbered paragraphs make it easier to study.

Promises. Promises. Promises.
Eugene H. Peterson
1-57683-466-2

Everybody's making promises these days.
But who's really true to their word?

God is. Take a look at His promises—promises of a real life and a future. See how knowing them can help you trust God even more.

The Message:
The Gospel of John
in Contemporary Language
Eugene H. Peterson
1-57683-432-8

Read what John witnessed as he walked alongside Jesus. Then help others find hope and a new way of life—better and more real than they've ever dreamed of experiencing. Share it with everyone you know!

1-800-366-7788
www.th1nkbooks.com

THINK

What if He were born in Bethlehem . . . Pennsylvania?

!HERO Comics and Graphic Novel

Comic 1: 1-57683-504-9
Comic 2: 1-57683-501-4
Comic 3: 1-57683-502-2
Comic 4: 1-57683-503-0
*Graphic Novel: 1-57683-500-6

*includes comics 1-4 plus the previously unreleased comic 5

Follow the !HERO action up close and personal! Read as Special Agent Alex Hunter strives to discover the story behind a mysterious miracle-worker from Bethlehem, Pennsylvania, whose very presence is changing the world.

In a series of five action-packed episodes, best-selling author Stephen R. Lawhead, collaborating with author and penciler Ross Lawhead, incites the imagination to wonder: What if He were born today? Collect all four comics, then pick up the graphic novel to get issue five!

Check out www.herouniverse.com for more information.

1-800-366-7788
www.th1nkbooks.com

ASSURANCE OF GOD'S LOVE NKJV
ZEPHANIAH 3:17

"The LORD your God in your midst,
The Mighty One, will save;
He will rejoice over you with gladness,
He will quiet you with His love,
He will rejoice over you with singing."

ZEPHANIAH 3:17

New Believer

ASSURANCE OF GOD'S LOVE NKJV
1 KINGS 8:23

And he said: "LORD God of Israel, there is no
God in heaven above or on earth below like
You, who keep Your covenant and mercy with
Your servants who walk before You with all
their heart."

1 KINGS 8:23

New Believer

ASSURANCE OF JESUS NKJV
MATTHEW 1:21

And she will bring forth a Son, and you shall
call His name JESUS, for He will save His people
from their sins.

MATTHEW 1:21

New Believer

ASSURANCE OF JESUS NKJV
HEBREWS 1:3

Who being the brightness of His glory and the
express image of His person, and upholding all
things by the word of His power, when He had
by Himself purged our sins, sat down at the
right hand of the Majesty on high.

HEBREWS 1:3

New Believer

ASSURANCE OF GOD'S LOVE NKJV
PSALM 86:5

For You, Lord, are good,
and ready to forgive,
And abundant in mercy to all those
who call upon You.

PSALM 86:5

New Believer

ASSURANCE OF GOD'S LOVE NKJV
ROMANS 5:5

Now hope does not disappoint, because the
love of God has been poured out in our hearts
by the Holy Spirit who was given to us.

ROMANS 5:5

New Believer

ASSURANCE OF JESUS NKJV
JOHN 14:6

Jesus said to him, "I am the way, the truth,
and the life. No one comes to the Father
except through Me."

JOHN 14:6

New Believer

ASSURANCE OF JESUS NKJV
LUKE 24:39-40

"Behold My hands and My feet, that it is I
Myself. Handle Me and see, for a spirit does
not have flesh and bones as you see I have."
When He had said this, He showed them His
hands and His feet.

LUKE 24:39-40

New Believer

ASSURANCE OF GOD'S LOVE
PSALM 86:5

KJV

For thou, Lord, art good, and ready to forgive; and plenteous in mercy unto all them that call upon thee.

PSALM 86:5

New Believer

ASSURANCE OF GOD'S LOVE
ZEPHANIAH 3:17

KJV

The LORD thy God in the midst of thee is mighty; he will save, he will rejoice over thee with joy; he will rest in his love, he will joy over thee with singing.

ZEPHANIAH 3:17

New Believer

ASSURANCE OF GOD'S LOVE
ROMANS 5:5

KJV

And hope maketh not ashamed; because the love of God is shed abroad in our hearts by the Holy Ghost which is given unto us.

ROMANS 5:5

New Believer

ASSURANCE OF GOD'S LOVE
1 KINGS 8:23

KJV

And he said, LORD God of Israel, there is no God like thee, in heaven above, or on earth beneath, who keepest covenant and mercy with thy servants that walk before thee with all their heart.

1 KINGS 8:23

New Believer

ASSURANCE OF JESUS
JOHN 14:6

KJV

Jesus saith unto him, I am the way, the truth, and the life: no man cometh unto the Father, but by me.

JOHN 14:6

New Believer

ASSURANCE OF JESUS
MATTHEW 1:21

KJV

And she shall bring forth a son, and thou shalt call his name JESUS: for he shall save his people from their sins.

MATTHEW 1:21

New Believer

ASSURANCE OF JESUS
LUKE 24:39-40

KJV

Behold my hands and my feet, that it is I myself: handle me, and see; for a spirit hath not flesh and bones, as ye see me have.
    And when he had thus spoken, he shewed them his hands and his feet.

LUKE 24:39-40

New Believer

ASSURANCE OF JESUS
HEBREWS 1:3

KJV

Who being the brightness of his glory, and the express image of his person, and upholding all things by the word of his power, when he had by himself purged our sins, sat down on the right hand of the Majesty on high.

HEBREWS 1:3

New Believer

ASSURANCE OF FORGIVENESS — NIV
Acts 10:43

All the prophets testify about him that everyone who believes in him receives forgiveness
of sins through his name.

Acts 10:43

New Believer

ASSURANCE OF FORGIVENESS — NIV
Isaiah 53:5

He was pierced for our transgressions,
    he was crushed for our iniquities;
the punishment that brought us peace was
        upon him,
    and by his wounds we are healed.

Isaiah 53:

New Believer

ASSURANCE OF FORGIVENESS — NIV
1 Peter 2:24

He himself bore our sins in his body on the
tree, so that we might die to sins and live for
righteousness; by his wounds you have been
healed.

1 Peter 2:24

New Believer

ASSURANCE OF FORGIVENESS — NIV
Ephesians 1:7-8

In him we have redemption through his blood,
the forgiveness of sins, in accordance with the
riches of God's grace that he lavished on us
with all wisdom and understanding.

Ephesians 1:7-8

New Believer

ASSURANCE OF STRENGTH — NIV
1 Corinthians 15:56-57

The sting of death is sin, and the power of sin
is the law. But thanks be to God! He gives us
the victory through our Lord Jesus Christ.

1 Corinthians 15:56-57

New Believer

ASSURANCE OF STRENGTH — NIV
2 Thessalonians 3:3

The Lord is faithful, and he will strengthen
and protect you from the evil one.

2 Thessalonians 3:3

New Believer

ASSURANCE OF STRENGTH — NIV
John 10:10

"The thief comes only to steal and kill and
destroy; I have come that they may have life,
and have it to the full."

John 10:10

New Believer

ASSURANCE OF STRENGTH — NIV
2 Peter 1:3

His divine power has given us everything we
need for life and godliness through our
knowledge of him who called us by his own
glory and goodness.

2 Peter 1:3

New Believer

ASSURANCE OF FORGIVENESS NLT
Isaiah 53:5

But he was wounded and crushed for our sins. He was beaten that we might have peace. He was whipped, and we were healed!

Isaiah 53:5

New Believer

ASSURANCE OF FORGIVENESS NLT
Ephesians 1:7-8

He is so rich in kindness that he purchased our freedom through the blood of his Son, and our sins are forgiven. He has showered his kindness on us, along with all wisdom and understanding.

Ephesians 1:7-8

New Believer

ASSURANCE OF STRENGTH NLT
2 Thessalonians 3:3

But the Lord is faithful; he will make you strong and guard you from the evil one.

2 Thessalonians 3:3

New Believer

ASSURANCE OF STRENGTH NLT
2 Peter 1:3

As we know Jesus better, his divine power gives us everything we need for living a godly life. He has called us to receive his own glory and goodness!

2 Peter 1:3

New Believer

ASSURANCE OF FORGIVENESS NLT
Acts 10:43

He is the one all the prophets testified about, saying that everyone who believes in him will have their sins forgiven through his name.

Acts 10:43

New Believer

ASSURANCE OF FORGIVENESS NLT
1 Peter 2:24

He personally carried away our sins in his own body on the cross so we can be dead to sin and live for what is right. You have been healed by his wounds!

1 Peter 2:24

New Believer

ASSURANCE OF STRENGTH NLT
1 Corinthians 15:56-57

For sin is the sting that results in death, and the law gives sin its power. How we thank God, who gives us victory over sin and death through Jesus Christ our Lord!

1 Corinthians 15:56-57

New Believer

ASSURANCE OF STRENGTH NLT
John 10:10

"The thief's purpose is to steal and kill and destroy. My purpose is to give life in all its fullness."

John 10:10

New Believer

ASSURANCE OF FORGIVENESS   KJV
Acts 10:43

To him give all the prophets witness, that through his name whosoever believeth in him shall receive remission of sins.

Acts 10:43

New Believer

ASSURANCE OF FORGIVENESS   KJV
Isaiah 53:5

But he was wounded for our transgressions, he was bruised for our iniquities: the chastisement of our peace was upon him; and with his stripes we are healed.

Isaiah 53:5

New Believer

ASSURANCE OF FORGIVENESS   KJV
1 Peter 2:24

Who his own self bare our sins in his own body on the tree, that we, being dead to sins, should live unto righteousness: by whose stripes ye were healed.

1 Peter 2:24

New Believer

ASSURANCE OF FORGIVENESS   KJV
Ephesians 1:7-8

In whom we have redemption through his blood, the forgiveness of sins, according to the riches of his grace;
    Wherein he hath abounded toward us in all wisdom and prudence.

Ephesians 1:7-8

New Believer

ASSURANCE OF STRENGTH   KJV
1 Corinthians 15:56-57

The sting of death is sin; and the strength of sin is the law.
    But thanks be to God, which giveth us the victory through our Lord Jesus Christ.

1 Corinthians 15:56-57

New Believer

ASSURANCE OF STRENGTH   KJV
2 Thessalonians 3:3

But the Lord is faithful, who shall stablish you, and keep you from evil.

2 Thessalonians 3:3

New Believer

ASSURANCE OF STRENGTH   KJV
John 10:10

The thief cometh not, but for to steal, and to kill, and to destroy: I am come that they might have life, and that they might have it more abundantly.

John 10:10

New Believer

ASSURANCE OF STRENGTH   KJV
2 Peter 1:3

According as his divine power hath given unto us all things that pertain unto life and godliness, through the knowledge of him that hath called us to glory and virtue.

2 Peter 1:3

New Believer

ASSURANCE OF FORGIVENESS · NKJV
ISAIAH 53:5

But He was wounded for our transgressions,
    He was bruised for our iniquities;
The chastisement for our peace was upon
    Him,
And by His stripes we are healed.

ISAIAH 53:5

New Believer

ASSURANCE OF FORGIVENESS · NKJV
ACTS 10:43

To Him all the prophets witness that, through His name, whoever believes in Him will receive remission of sins.

ACTS 10:43

New Believer

ASSURANCE OF FORGIVENESS · NKJV
EPHESIANS 1:7-8

In Him we have redemption through His blood, the forgiveness of sins, according to the riches of His grace which He made to abound toward us in all wisdom and prudence.

EPHESIANS 1:7-8

New Believer

ASSURANCE OF FORGIVENESS · NKJV
1 PETER 2:24

Who Himself bore our sins in His own body on the tree, that we, having died to sins, might live for righteousness—by whose stripes you were healed.

1 PETER 2:24

New Believer

ASSURANCE OF STRENGTH · NKJV
2 THESSALONIANS 3:3

But the Lord is faithful, who will establish you and guard you from the evil one.

2 THESSALONIANS 3:3

New Believer

ASSURANCE OF STRENGTH · NKJV
1 CORINTHIANS 15:56-57

The sting of death is sin, and the strength of sin is the law.
    But thanks be to God, who gives us the victory through our Lord Jesus Christ.

1 CORINTHIANS 15:56-57

New Believer

ASSURANCE OF STRENGTH · NKJV
2 PETER 1:3

As His divine power has given to us all things that pertain to life and godliness, through the knowledge of Him who called us by glory and virtue.

2 PETER 1:3

New Believer

ASSURANCE OF STRENGTH · NKJV
JOHN 10:10

"The thief does not come except to steal, and to kill, and to destroy. I have come that they may have life, and that they may have it more abundantly."

JOHN 10:10

New Believer

ASSURANCE OF AN ANSWER NIV
JOHN 16:24

"Until now you have not asked for anything in my name. Ask and you will receive, and your joy will be complete."

JOHN 16:24

New Believer

ASSURANCE OF AN ANSWER NIV
MATTHEW 7:7-8

"Ask and it will be given to you; seek and you will find; knock and the door will be opened to you. For everyone who asks receives; he who seeks finds; and to him who knocks, the door will be opened."

MATTHEW 7:7-8

New Believer

ASSURANCE OF AN ANSWER NIV
JEREMIAH 33:3

"Call to me and I will answer you and tell you great and unsearchable things you do not know."

JEREMIAH 33:3

New Believer

ASSURANCE OF AN ANSWER NIV
1 JOHN 5:14

This is the confidence we have in approaching God: that if we ask anything according to his will, he hears us.

1 JOHN 5:14

New Believer

ASSURANCE OF ETERNAL LIFE NIV
1 JOHN 5:11-12

This is the testimony: God has given us eternal life, and this life is in his Son. He who has the Son has life; he who does not have the Son of God does not have life.

1 JOHN 5:11-12

New Believer

ASSURANCE OF ETERNAL LIFE NIV
HEBREWS 2:14-15

Since the children have flesh and blood, he too shared in their humanity so that by his death he might destroy him who holds the power of death—that is, the devil—and free those who all their lives were held in slavery by their fear of death.

HEBREWS 2:14-15

New Believer

ASSURANCE OF ETERNAL LIFE NIV
JOHN 3:16

"God so loved the world that he gave his one and only Son, that whoever believes in him shall not perish but have eternal life."

JOHN 3:16

New Believer

ASSURANCE OF ETERNAL LIFE NIV
1 JOHN 2:17

The world and its desires pass away, but the man who does the will of God lives forever.

1 JOHN 2:17

New Believer

ASSURANCE OF AN ANSWER _{NLT}
MATTHEW 7:7-8

"Keep on asking, and you will be given what you ask for. Keep on looking, and you will find. Keep on knocking, and the door will be opened. For everyone who asks, receives. Everyone who seeks, finds. And the door is opened to everyone who knocks."

MATTHEW 7:7-8

New Believer

ASSURANCE OF AN ANSWER _{NLT}
JOHN 16:24

"You haven't done this before. Ask, using my name, and you will receive, and you will have abundant joy."

JOHN 16:24

New Believer

ASSURANCE OF AN ANSWER _{NLT}
1 JOHN 5:14

And we can be confident that he will listen to us whenever we ask him for anything in line with his will.

1 JOHN 5:14

New Believer

ASSURANCE OF AN ANSWER _{NLT}
JEREMIAH 33:3

"Ask me and I will tell you some remarkable secrets about what is going to happen here."

JEREMIAH 33:3

New Believer

ASSURANCE OF ETERNAL LIFE _{NLT}
HEBREWS 2:14-15

Because God's children are human beings—made of flesh and blood—Jesus also became flesh and blood by being born in human form. For only as a human being could he die, and only by dying could he break the power of the Devil, who had the power of death. Only in this way could he deliver those who have lived all their lives as slaves to the fear of dying.

HEBREWS 2:14-15

New Believer

ASSURANCE OF ETERNAL LIFE _{NLT}
1 JOHN 5:11-12

And this is what God has testified: He has given us eternal life, and this life is in his Son. So whoever has God's Son has life; whoever does not have his Son does not have life.

1 JOHN 5:11-12

New Believer

ASSURANCE OF ETERNAL LIFE _{NLT}
1 JOHN 2:17

And this world is fading away, along with everything it craves. But if you do the will of God, you will live forever.

1 JOHN 2:17

New Believer

ASSURANCE OF ETERNAL LIFE _{NLT}
JOHN 3:16

"For God so loved the world that he gave his only Son, so that everyone who believes in him will not perish but have eternal life."

JOHN 3:16

New Believer

New Believer

ASSURANCE OF AN ANSWER KJV
JOHN 16:24

Hitherto have ye asked nothing in my name: ask, and ye shall receive, that your joy may be full.

JOHN 16:24

New Believer

ASSURANCE OF AN ANSWER KJV
MATTHEW 7:7-8

Ask, and it shall be given you; seek, and ye shall find; knock, and it shall be opened unto you:
For every one that asketh receiveth; and he that seeketh findeth; and to him that knocketh it shall be opened.

MATTHEW 7:7-8

New Believer

ASSURANCE OF AN ANSWER KJV
JEREMIAH 33:3

Call unto me, and I will answer thee, and shew thee great and mighty things, which thou knowest not.

JEREMIAH 33:3

New Believer

ASSURANCE OF AN ANSWER KJV
1 JOHN 5:14

And this is the confidence that we have in him, that, if we ask any thing according to his will, he heareth us.

1 JOHN 5:14

New Believer

ASSURANCE OF ETERNAL LIFE KJV
1 JOHN 5:11-12

And this is the record, that God hath given to us eternal life, and this life is in his Son.
He that hath the Son hath life; and he that hath not the Son of God hath not life.

1 JOHN 5:11-12

New Believer

ASSURANCE OF ETERNAL LIFE KJV
HEBREWS 2:14-15

Forasmuch then as the children are partakers of flesh and blood, he also himself likewise took part of the same; that through death he might destroy him that had the power of death, that is, the devil;
And deliver them who through fear of death were all their lifetime subject to bondage.

HEBREWS 2:14-15

New Believer

ASSURANCE OF ETERNAL LIFE KJV
JOHN 3:16

For God so loved the world, that he gave his only begotten Son, that whosoever believeth in him should not perish, but have everlasting life.

JOHN 3:16

New Believer

ASSURANCE OF ETERNAL LIFE KJV
1 JOHN 2:17

And the world passeth away, and the lust thereof: but he that doeth the will of God abideth for ever.

1 JOHN 2:17

New Believer

ASSURANCE OF AN ANSWER NKJV
MATTHEW 7:7-8

"Ask, and it will be given to you; seek, and you will find; knock, and it will be opened to you.
"For everyone who asks receives, and he who seeks finds, and to him who knocks it will be opened."

MATTHEW 7:7-8

New Believer

ASSURANCE OF AN ANSWER NKJV
JOHN 16:24

"Until now you have asked nothing in My name. Ask, and you will receive, that your joy may be full."

JOHN 16:24

New Believer

ASSURANCE OF AN ANSWER NKJV
1 JOHN 5:14

Now this is the confidence that we have in Him, that if we ask anything according to His will, He hears us.

1 JOHN 5:14

New Believer

ASSURANCE OF AN ANSWER NKJV
JEREMIAH 33:3

"Call to Me, and I will answer you, and show you great and mighty things, which you do not know."

JEREMIAH 33:3

New Believer

ASSURANCE OF ETERNAL LIFE NKJV
HEBREWS 2:14-15

Inasmuch then as the children have partaken of flesh and blood, He Himself likewise shared in the same, that through death He might destroy him who had the power of death, that is, the devil, and release those who through fear of death were all their lifetime subject to bondage.

HEBREWS 2:14-15

New Believer

ASSURANCE OF ETERNAL LIFE NKJV
1 JOHN 5:11-12

And this is the testimony: that God has given us eternal life, and this life is in His Son.
He who has the Son has life; he who does not have the Son of God does not have life.

1 JOHN 5:11-12

New Believer

ASSURANCE OF ETERNAL LIFE NKJV
1 JOHN 2:17

And the world is passing away, and the lust of it; but he who does the will of God abides forever.

1 JOHN 2:17

New Believer

ASSURANCE OF ETERNAL LIFE NKJV
JOHN 3:16

"For God so loved the world that He gave His only begotten Son, that whoever believes in Him should not perish but have everlasting life."

JOHN 3:16

New Believer

ASSURANCE OF GUIDANCE
PROVERBS 3:5-6

NIV

Trust in the LORD with all your heart
and lean not on your own understanding;
in all your ways acknowledge him,
and he will make your paths straight.

PROVERBS 3:5-6

New Believer

ASSURANCE OF GUIDANCE
PSALM 32:8

NIV

I will instruct you and teach you in the way
you should go;
I will counsel you and watch over you.

PSALM 32:8

New Believer

ASSURANCE OF GUIDANCE
JEREMIAH 17:7

NIV

"Blessed is the man who trusts in the LORD,
whose confidence is in him."

JEREMIAH 17:7

New Believer

ASSURANCE OF GUIDANCE
1 JOHN 4:4

NIV

You, dear children, are from God and have
overcome them, because the one who is in
you is greater than the one who is in the
world.

1 JOHN 4:4

New Believer

DISCIPLE OF GOD
MATTHEW 22:37

NIV

"'Love the Lord your God with all your heart
and with all your soul and with all your
mind.'"

MATTHEW 22:37

Growing Disciple

DISCIPLE OF GOD
DEUTERONOMY 7:9

NIV

Know therefore that the LORD your God is God;
he is the faithful God, keeping his covenant of
love to a thousand generations of those who
love him and keep his commands.

DEUTERONOMY 7:9

Growing Disciple

DISCIPLE OF GOD
1 CORINTHIANS 10:31

NIV

Whether you eat or drink or whatever you do,
do it all for the glory of God.

1 CORINTHIANS 10:31

Growing Disciple

DISCIPLE OF GOD
1 CHRONICLES 29:11

NIV

Yours, O LORD, is the greatness and the power
and the glory and the majesty and the
splendor,
for everything in heaven and earth is yours.
Yours, O LORD, is the kingdom;
you are exalted as head over all.

1 CHRONICLES 29:11

Growing Disciple

ASSURANCE OF GUIDANCE · NLT
PSALM 32:8

The LORD says, "I will guide you along the best
pathway for your life.
I will advise you and watch over you."

PSALM 32:8

New Believer

ASSURANCE OF GUIDANCE · NLT
1 JOHN 4:4

But you belong to God, my dear children. You
have already won your fight with these false
prophets, because the Spirit who lives in you
is greater than the spirit who lives in the
world.

1 JOHN 4:4

New Believer

DISCIPLE OF GOD · NLT
DEUTERONOMY 7:9

Understand, therefore, that the LORD your God
is indeed God. He is the faithful God who
keeps his covenant for a thousand generations
and constantly loves those who love him and
obey his commands.

DEUTERONOMY 7:9

Growing Disciple

DISCIPLE OF GOD · NLT
1 CHRONICLES 29:11

Yours, O LORD, is the greatness, the power, the
glory, the victory, and the majesty. Everything
in the heavens and on earth is yours, O LORD,
and this is your kingdom. We adore you as the
one who is over all things.

1 CHRONICLES 29:11

Growing Disciple

ASSURANCE OF GUIDANCE · NLT
PROVERBS 3:5-6

Trust in the LORD with all your heart; do not
depend on your own understanding. Seek his
will in all you do, and he will direct your
paths.

PROVERBS 3:5-6

New Believer

ASSURANCE OF GUIDANCE · NLT
JEREMIAH 17:7

"But blessed are those who trust in the LORD
and have made the LORD their hope and confidence."

JEREMIAH 17:7

New Believer

DISCIPLE OF GOD · NLT
MATTHEW 22:37

Jesus replied, "'You must love the Lord your
God with all your heart, all your soul, and all
your mind.'"

MATTHEW 22:37

Growing Disciple

DISCIPLE OF GOD · NLT
1 CORINTHIANS 10:31

Whatever you eat or drink or whatever you
do, you must do all for the glory of God.

1 CORINTHIANS 10:31

Growing Disciple

ASSURANCE OF GUIDANCE KJV
PROVERBS 3:5-6

Trust in the LORD with all thine heart; and lean not unto thine own understanding.
In all thy ways acknowledge him, and he shall direct thy paths.

PROVERBS 3:5-6

New Believer

ASSURANCE OF GUIDANCE KJV
PSALM 32:8

I will instruct thee and teach thee in the way which thou shalt go: I will guide thee with mine eye.

PSALM 32:8

New Believer

ASSURANCE OF GUIDANCE KJV
JEREMIAH 17:7

Blessed is the man that trusteth in the LORD, and whose hope the LORD is.

JEREMIAH 17:7

New Believer

ASSURANCE OF GUIDANCE KJV
1 JOHN 4:4

Ye are of God, little children, and have overcome them: because greater is he that is in you, than he that is in the world.

1 JOHN 4:4

New Believer

DISCIPLE OF GOD KJV
MATTHEW 22:37

Jesus said unto him, Thou shalt love the Lord thy God with all thy heart, and with all thy soul, and with all thy mind.

MATTHEW 22:37

Growing Disciple

DISCIPLE OF GOD KJV
DEUTERONOMY 7:9

Know therefore that the LORD thy God, he is God, the faithful God, which keepeth covenant and mercy with them that love him and keep his commandments to a thousand generations.

DEUTERONOMY 7:9

Growing Disciple

DISCIPLE OF GOD KJV
1 CORINTHIANS 10:31

Whether therefore ye eat, or drink, or whatsoever ye do, do all to the glory of God.

1 CORINTHIANS 10:31

Growing Disciple

DISCIPLE OF GOD KJV
1 CHRONICLES 29:11

Thine, O LORD, is the greatness, and the power, and the glory, and the victory, and the majesty: for all that is in the heaven and in the earth is thine; thine is the kingdom, O LORD, and thou art exalted as head above all.

1 CHRONICLES 29:11

Growing Disciple

ASSURANCE OF GUIDANCE   NKJV
PSALM 32:8

I will instruct you and teach you in the way
    you should go;
I will guide you with My eye.

PSALM 32:8

New Believer

ASSURANCE OF GUIDANCE   NKJV
1 JOHN 4:4

You are of God, little children, and have overcome them, because He who is in you is
greater than he who is in the world.

1 JOHN 4:4

New Believer

DISCIPLE OF GOD   NKJV
DEUTERONOMY 7:9

Therefore know that the LORD your God, He is
God, the faithful God who keeps covenant
and mercy for a thousand generations with
those who love Him and keep His commandments.

DEUTERONOMY 7:9

Growing Disciple

DISCIPLE OF GOD   NKJV
1 CHRONICLES 29:11

Yours, O LORD, is the greatness,
The power and the glory,
The victory and the majesty;
For all that is in heaven
    and in earth is Yours;
Yours is the kingdom, O LORD,
And You are exalted as head over all.

1 CHRONICLES 29:11

Growing Disciple

ASSURANCE OF GUIDANCE   NKJV
PROVERBS 3:5-6

Trust in the LORD with all your heart,
And lean not on your own understanding;
In all your ways acknowledge Him,
And He shall direct your paths.

PROVERBS 3:5-6

New Believer

ASSURANCE OF GUIDANCE   NKJV
JEREMIAH 17:7

"Blessed is the man who trusts in the LORD,
And whose hope is the LORD."

JEREMIAH 17:7

New Believer

DISCIPLE OF GOD   NKJV
MATTHEW 22:37

Jesus said to him, "'You shall love the LORD
your God with all your heart, with all your
soul, and with all your mind.'"

MATTHEW 22:37

Growing Disciple

DISCIPLE OF GOD   NKJV
1 CORINTHIANS 10:31

Therefore, whether you eat or drink, or whatever you do, do all to the glory of God.

1 CORINTHIANS 10:31

Growing Disciple

DISCIPLE OF CHRIST NIV
1 JOHN 2:6

Whoever claims to live in him must walk as Jesus did.

1 JOHN 2:6

Growing Disciple

DISCIPLE OF CHRIST NIV
1 CORINTHIANS 15:22

As in Adam all die, so in Christ all will be made alive.

1 CORINTHIANS 15:22

Growing Disciple

DISCIPLE OF CHRIST NIV
PHILIPPIANS 2:10-11

At the name of Jesus every knee should bow,
    in heaven and on earth and under the earth,
and every tongue confess that Jesus Christ is
        Lord,
    to the glory of God the Father.

PHILIPPIANS 2:10-11

Growing Disciple

DISCIPLE OF CHRIST NIV
COLOSSIANS 2:6

Just as you received Christ Jesus as Lord, continue to live in him.

COLOSSIANS 2:6

Growing Disciple

DISCIPLE OF THE WORD NIV
COLOSSIANS 3:16

Let the word of Christ dwell in you richly as you teach and admonish one another with all wisdom, and as you sing psalms, hymns and spiritual songs with gratitude in your hearts to God.

COLOSSIANS 3:16

Growing Disciple

DISCIPLE OF THE WORD NIV
ROMANS 15:4

Everything that was written in the past was written to teach us, so that through endurance and the encouragement of the Scriptures we might have hope.

ROMANS 15:4

Growing Disciple

DISCIPLE OF THE WORD NIV
DEUTERONOMY 11:18-19

Fix these words of mine in your hearts and minds; tie them as symbols on your hands and bind them on your foreheads. Teach them to your children, talking about them when you sit at home and when you walk along the road, when you lie down and when you get up.

DEUTERONOMY 11:18-19

Growing Disciple

DISCIPLE OF THE WORD NIV
JAMES 1:22

Do not merely listen to the word, and so deceive yourselves. Do what it says.

JAMES 1:22

Growing Disciple

DISCIPLE OF CHRIST NLT
1 CORINTHIANS 15:22

Everyone dies because all of us are related to Adam, the first man. But all who are related to Christ, the other man, will be given new life.

1 CORINTHIANS 15:22

Growing Disciple

DISCIPLE OF CHRIST NLT
COLOSSIANS 2:6

And now, just as you accepted Christ Jesus as your Lord, you must continue to live in obedience to him.

COLOSSIANS 2:6

Growing Disciple

DISCIPLE OF THE WORD NLT
ROMANS 15:4

Such things were written in the Scriptures long ago to teach us. They give us hope and encouragement as we wait patiently for God's promises.

ROMANS 15:4

Growing Disciple

DISCIPLE OF THE WORD NLT
JAMES 1:22

And remember, it is a message to obey, not just to listen to. If you don't obey, you are only fooling yourself.

JAMES 1:22

Growing Disciple

DISCIPLE OF CHRIST NLT
1 JOHN 2:6

Those who say they live in God should live their lives as Christ did.

1 JOHN 2:6

Growing Disciple

DISCIPLE OF CHRIST NLT
PHILIPPIANS 2:10-11

So that at the name of Jesus every knee will bow, in heaven and on earth and under the earth, and every tongue will confess that Jesus Christ is Lord, to the glory of God the Father.

PHILIPPIANS 2:10-11

Growing Disciple

DISCIPLE OF THE WORD NLT
COLOSSIANS 3:16

Let the words of Christ, in all their richness, live in your hearts and make you wise. Use his words to teach and counsel each other. Sing psalms and hymns and spiritual songs to God with thankful hearts.

COLOSSIANS 3:16

Growing Disciple

DISCIPLE OF THE WORD NLT
DEUTERONOMY 11:18-19

So commit yourselves completely to these words of mine. Tie them to your hands as a reminder, and wear them on your forehead. Teach them to your children. Talk about them when you are at home and when you are away on a journey, when you are lying down and when you are getting up again.

DEUTERONOMY 11:18-19

Growing Disciple

DISCIPLE OF CHRIST
1 JOHN 2:6
KJV

He that saith he abideth in him ought himself also so to walk, even as he walked.

1 JOHN 2:6

Growing Disciple

DISCIPLE OF CHRIST
1 CORINTHIANS 15:22
KJV

For as in Adam all die, even so in Christ shall all be made alive.

1 CORINTHIANS 15:22

Growing Disciple

DISCIPLE OF CHRIST
PHILIPPIANS 2:10-11
KJV

That at the name of Jesus every knee should bow, of things in heaven, and things in earth, and things under the earth;
And that every tongue should confess that Jesus Christ is Lord, to the glory of God the Father.

PHILIPPIANS 2:10-11

Growing Disciple

DISCIPLE OF CHRIST
COLOSSIANS 2:6
KJV

As ye have therefore received Christ Jesus the Lord, so walk ye in him.

COLOSSIANS 2:6

Growing Disciple

DISCIPLE OF THE WORD
COLOSSIANS 3:16
KJV

Let the word of Christ dwell in you richly in all wisdom; teaching and admonishing one another in psalms and hymns and spiritual songs, singing with grace in your hearts to the Lord.

COLOSSIANS 3:16

Growing Disciple

DISCIPLE OF THE WORD
ROMANS 15:4
KJV

For whatsoever things were written aforetime were written for our learning, that we through patience and comfort of the scriptures might have hope.

ROMANS 15:4

Growing Disciple

DISCIPLE OF THE WORD
DEUTERONOMY 11:18-19
KJV

Therefore shall ye lay up these my words in your heart and in your soul, and bind them for a sign upon your hand, that they may be as frontlets between your eyes.
And ye shall teach them your children, speaking of them when thou sittest in thine house, and when thou walkest by the way, when thou liest down, and when thou risest up.

DEUTERONOMY 11:18-19

Growing Disciple

DISCIPLE OF THE WORD
JAMES 1:22
KJV

But be ye doers of the word, and not hearers only, deceiving your own selves.

JAMES 1:22

Growing Disciple

DISCIPLE OF CHRIST NKJV
1 CORINTHIANS 15:22

For as in Adam all die, even so in Christ all shall be made alive.

1 CORINTHIANS 15:22

Growing Disciple

DISCIPLE OF CHRIST NKJV
COLOSSIANS 2:6

As you therefore have received Christ Jesus the Lord, so walk in Him.

COLOSSIANS 2:6

Growing Disciple

DISCIPLE OF THE WORD NKJV
ROMANS 15:4

For whatever things were written before were written for our learning, that we through the patience and comfort of the Scriptures might have hope.

ROMANS 15:4

Growing Disciple

DISCIPLE OF THE WORD NKJV
JAMES 1:22

But be doers of the word, and not hearers only, deceiving yourselves.

JAMES 1:22

Growing Disciple

DISCIPLE OF CHRIST NKJV
1 JOHN 2:6

He who says he abides in Him ought himself also to walk just as He walked.

1 JOHN 2:6

Growing Disciple

DISCIPLE OF CHRIST NKJV
PHILIPPIANS 2:10-11

That at the name of Jesus every knee should bow, of those in heaven, and of those on earth, and of those under the earth, and that every tongue should confess that Jesus Christ is Lord, to the glory of God the Father.

PHILIPPIANS 2:10-11

Growing Disciple

DISCIPLE OF THE WORD NKJV
COLOSSIANS 3:16

Let the word of Christ dwell in you richly in all wisdom, teaching and admonishing one another in psalms and hymns and spiritual songs, singing with grace in your hearts to the Lord.

COLOSSIANS 3:16

Growing Disciple

DISCIPLE OF THE WORD NKJV
DEUTERONOMY 11:18-19

Therefore you shall lay up these words of mine in your heart and in your soul, and bind them as a sign on your hand, and they shall be as frontlets between your eyes.

You shall teach them to your children, speaking of them when you sit in your house, when you walk by the way, when you lie down, and when you rise up.

DEUTERONOMY 11:18-19

Growing Disciple

DISCIPLE OF OTHERS
PSALM 122:1 — NIV

I rejoiced with those who said to me,
"Let us go to the house of the LORD."

PSALM 122:1

Growing Disciple

DISCIPLE OF OTHERS
ECCLESIASTES 4:9-10 — NIV

Two are better than one,
because they have a good return for their
work:
If one falls down,
his friend can help him up.
But pity the man who falls
and has no one to help him up!

ECCLESIASTES 4:9-10

Growing Disciple

DISCIPLE OF OTHERS
ROMANS 12:4-5 — NIV

Just as each of us has one body with many
members, and these members do not all have
the same function, so in Christ we who are
many form one body, and each member
belongs to all the others.

ROMANS 12:4-5

Growing Disciple

DISCIPLE OF OTHERS
PROVERBS 19:20 — NIV

Listen to advice and accept instruction,
and in the end you will be wise.

PROVERBS 19:20

Growing Disciple

DISCIPLE OF LIFE
DEUTERONOMY 26:16 — NIV

The LORD your God commands you this day to
follow these decrees and laws; carefully
observe them with all your heart and with all
your soul.

DEUTERONOMY 26:16

Growing Disciple

DISCIPLE OF LIFE
1 TIMOTHY 4:8 — NIV

Physical training is of some value, but godliness has value for all things, holding promise
for both the present life and the life to come.

1 TIMOTHY 4:8

Growing Disciple

DISCIPLE OF LIFE
COLOSSIANS 3:23 — NIV

Whatever you do, work at it with all your
heart, as working for the Lord, not for men.

COLOSSIANS 3:23

Growing Disciple

DISCIPLE OF LIFE
1 CORINTHIANS 9:24 — NIV

Do you not know that in a race all the runners
run, but only one gets the prize? Run in such
a way as to get the prize.

1 CORINTHIANS 9:24

Growing Disciple

DISCIPLE OF OTHERS
NLT
ECCLESIASTES 4:9-10

Two people can accomplish more than twice as much as one; they get a better return for their labor. If one person falls, the other can reach out and help. But people who are alone when they fall are in real trouble.

ECCLESIASTES 4:9-10

Growing Disciple

DISCIPLE OF OTHERS
NLT
PROVERBS 19:20

Get all the advice and instruction you can, and be wise the rest of your life.

PROVERBS 19:20

Growing Disciple

DISCIPLE OF LIFE
NLT
1 TIMOTHY 4:8

Physical exercise has some value, but spiritual exercise is much more important, for it promises a reward in both this life and the next.

1 TIMOTHY 4:8

Growing Disciple

DISCIPLE OF LIFE
NLT
1 CORINTHIANS 9:24

Remember that in a race everyone runs, but only one person gets the prize. You also must run in such a way that you will win.

1 CORINTHIANS 9:24

Growing Disciple

DISCIPLE OF OTHERS
NLT
PSALM 122:1

I was glad when they said to me,
"Let us go to the house of the LORD."

PSALM 122:1

Growing Disciple

DISCIPLE OF OTHERS
NLT
ROMANS 12:4-5

Just as our bodies have many parts and each part has a special function, so it is with Christ's body. We are all parts of his one body, and each of us has different work to do. And since we are all one body in Christ, we belong to each other, and each of us needs all the others.

ROMANS 12:4-5

Growing Disciple

DISCIPLE OF LIFE
NLT
DEUTERONOMY 26:16

Today the LORD your God has commanded you to obey all these laws and regulations. You must commit yourself to them without reservation.

DEUTERONOMY 26:16

Growing Disciple

DISCIPLE OF LIFE
NLT
COLOSSIANS 3:23

Work hard and cheerfully at whatever you do, as though you were working for the Lord rather than for people.

COLOSSIANS 3:23

Growing Disciple

DISCIPLE OF OTHERS

KJV

PSALM 122:1

I was glad when they said unto me, Let us go into the house of the LORD.

PSALM 122:1

Growing Disciple

DISCIPLE OF OTHERS

KJV

ROMANS 12:4-5

For as we have many members in one body, and all members have not the same office:

So we, being many, are one body in Christ, and every one members one of another.

ROMANS 12:4-5

Growing Disciple

DISCIPLE OF LIFE

KJV

DEUTERONOMY 26:16

This day the LORD thy God hath commanded thee to do these statutes and judgments: thou shalt therefore keep and do them with all thine heart, and with all thy soul.

DEUTERONOMY 26:16

Growing Disciple

DISCIPLE OF LIFE

KJV

COLOSSIANS 3:23

And whatsoever ye do, do it heartily, as to the Lord, and not unto men.

COLOSSIANS 3:23

Growing Disciple

DISCIPLE OF OTHERS

KJV

ECCLESIASTES 4:9-10

Two are better than one; because they have a good reward for their labour.

For if they fall, the one will lift up his fellow: but woe to him that is alone when he falleth; for he hath not another to help him up.

ECCLESIASTES 4:9-10

Growing Disciple

DISCIPLE OF OTHERS

KJV

PROVERBS 19:20

Hear counsel, and receive instruction, that thou mayest be wise in thy latter end.

PROVERBS 19:20

Growing Disciple

DISCIPLE OF LIFE

KJV

1 TIMOTHY 4:8

For bodily exercise profiteth little: but godliness is profitable unto all things, having promise of the life that now is, and of that which is to come.

1 TIMOTHY 4:8

Growing Disciple

DISCIPLE OF LIFE

KJV

1 CORINTHIANS 9:24

Know ye not that they which run in a race run all, but one receiveth the prize? So run, that ye may obtain.

1 CORINTHIANS 9:24

Growing Disciple

DISCIPLE OF OTHERS
NKJV
ECCLESIASTES 4:9-10

Two are better than one,
Because they have a good reward for their labor.
For if they fall,
    one will lift up his companion.
But woe to him who is alone when he falls,
For he has no one to help him up.

ECCLESIASTES 4:9-10

Growing Disciple

DISCIPLE OF OTHERS
NKJV
PROVERBS 19:20

Listen to counsel and receive instruction,
    That you may be wise in your latter days.

PROVERBS 19:20

Growing Disciple

DISCIPLE OF LIFE
NKJV
1 TIMOTHY 4:8

For bodily exercise profits a little, but godliness is profitable for all things, having promise of the life that now is and of that which is to come.

1 TIMOTHY 4:8

Growing Disciple

DISCIPLE OF LIFE
NKJV
1 CORINTHIANS 9:24

Do you not know that those who run in a race all run, but one receives the prize? Run in such a way that you may obtain it.

1 CORINTHIANS 9:24

Growing Disciple

DISCIPLE OF OTHERS
NKJV
PSALM 122:1

I was glad when they said to me,
    "Let us go into the house of the LORD."

PSALM 122:1

Growing Disciple

DISCIPLE OF OTHERS
NKJV
ROMANS 12:4-5

For as we have many members in one body, but all the members do not have the same function, so we, being many, are one body in Christ, and individually members of one another.

ROMANS 12:4-5

Growing Disciple

DISCIPLE OF LIFE
NKJV
DEUTERONOMY 26:16

This day the LORD your God commands you to observe these statutes and judgments; therefore you shall be careful to observe them with all your heart and with all your soul.

DEUTERONOMY 26:16

Growing Disciple

DISCIPLE OF LIFE
NKJV
COLOSSIANS 3:23

And whatever you do, do it heartily, as to the Lord and not to men.

COLOSSIANS 3:23

Growing Disciple

DISCIPLE FOR CHRIST NIV
1 JOHN 3:18

Dear children, let us not love with words or tongue but with actions and in truth.

1 JOHN 3:18

Growing Disciple

DISCIPLE FOR CHRIST NIV
1 CORINTHIANS 2:4-5

My message and my preaching were not with wise and persuasive words, but with a demonstration of the Spirit's power, so that your faith might not rest on men's wisdom, but on God's power.

1 CORINTHIANS 2:4-5

Growing Disciple

DISCIPLE FOR CHRIST NIV
COLOSSIANS 4:5

Be wise in the way you act toward outsiders; make the most of every opportunity.

COLOSSIANS 4:5

Growing Disciple

DISCIPLE FOR CHRIST NIV
1 TIMOTHY 4:12

Don't let anyone look down on you because you are young, but set an example for the believers in speech, in life, in love, in faith and in purity.

1 TIMOTHY 4:12

Growing Disciple

LOVE NIV
JAMES 1:19-20

My dear brothers, take note of this: Everyone should be quick to listen, slow to speak and slow to become angry, for man's anger does not bring about the righteous life that God desires.

JAMES 1:19-20

Life Issues

LOVE NIV
PSALM 89:1-2

I will sing of the LORD's great love forever;
    with my mouth I will make your faithfulness known through all generations.
I will declare that your love stands firm forever,
    that you established your faithfulness in heaven itself.

PSALM 89:1-2

Life Issues

LOVE NIV
1 JOHN 4:11

Dear friends, since God so loved us, we also ought to love one another.

1 JOHN 4:11

Life Issues

LOVE NIV
JOHN 15:17

"This is my command: Love each other."

JOHN 15:17

Life Issues

Growing Disciple / Life Issues

DISCIPLE FOR CHRIST   NLT
1 CORINTHIANS 2:4-5

And my message and my preaching were very plain. I did not use wise and persuasive speeches, but the Holy Spirit was powerful among you. I did this so that you might trust the power of God rather than human wisdom.

1 CORINTHIANS 2:4-5

Growing Disciple

DISCIPLE FOR CHRIST   NLT
1 TIMOTHY 4:12

Don't let anyone think less of you because you are young. Be an example to all believers in what you teach, in the way you live, in your love, your faith, and your purity.

1 TIMOTHY 4:12

Growing Disciple

LOVE   NLT
PSALM 89:1-2

I will sing of the tender mercies of the LORD forever!
Young and old will hear of your faithfulness. Your unfailing love will last forever.
Your faithfulness is as enduring as the heavens.

PSALM 89:1-2

Life Issues

LOVE   NLT
JOHN 15:17

"I command you to love each other."

JOHN 15:17

Life Issues

DISCIPLE FOR CHRIST   NLT
1 JOHN 3:18

Dear children, let us stop just saying we love each other; let us really show it by our actions.

1 JOHN 3:18

Growing Disciple

DISCIPLE FOR CHRIST   NLT
COLOSSIANS 4:5

Live wisely among those who are not Christians, and make the most of every opportunity.

COLOSSIANS 4:5

Growing Disciple

LOVE   NLT
JAMES 1:19-20

My dear brothers and sisters, be quick to listen, slow to speak, and slow to get angry. Your anger can never make things right in God's sight.

JAMES 1:19-20

Life Issues

LOVE   NLT
1 JOHN 4:11

Dear friends, since God loved us that much, we surely ought to love each other.

1 JOHN 4:11

Life Issues

GROWING DISCIPLE/LIFE ISSUES

DISCIPLE FOR CHRIST — KJV
1 John 3:18

My little children, let us not love in word, neither in tongue; but in deed and in truth.

1 John 3:18

Growing Disciple

DISCIPLE FOR CHRIST — KJV
1 Corinthians 2:4-5

And my speech and my preaching was not with enticing words of man's wisdom, but in demonstration of the Spirit and of power:

That your faith should not stand in the wisdom of men, but in the power of God.

1 Corinthians 2:4-5

Growing Disciple

DISCIPLE FOR CHRIST — KJV
Colossians 4:5

Walk in wisdom toward them that are without, redeeming the time.

Colossians 4:5

Growing Disciple

DISCIPLE FOR CHRIST — KJV
1 Timothy 4:12

Let no man despise thy youth; but be thou an example of the believers, in word, in conversation, in charity, in spirit, in faith, in purity.

1 Timothy 4:12

Growing Disciple

LOVE — KJV
James 1:19-20

Wherefore, my beloved brethren, let every man be swift to hear, slow to speak, slow to wrath:

For the wrath of man worketh not the righteousness of God.

James 1:19-20

Life Issues

LOVE — KJV
Psalm 89:1-2

I will sing of the mercies of the Lord for ever: with my mouth will I make known thy faithfulness to all generations.

For I have said, Mercy shall be built up for ever: thy faithfulness shalt thou establish in the very heavens.

Psalm 89:1-2

Life Issues

LOVE — KJV
1 John 4:11

Beloved, if God so loved us, we ought also to love one another.

1 John 4:11

Life Issues

LOVE — KJV
John 15:17

These things I command you, that ye love one another.

John 15:17

Life Issues

DISCIPLE FOR CHRIST
NKJV
1 CORINTHIANS 2:4-5

And my speech and my preaching were not
with persuasive words of human wisdom, but
in demonstration of the Spirit and of power,
that your faith should not be in the wisdom
of men but in the power of God.

1 CORINTHIANS 2:4-5

Growing Disciple

DISCIPLE FOR CHRIST
NKJV
1 JOHN 3:18

My little children, let us not love in word or in
tongue, but in deed and in truth.

1 JOHN 3:18

Growing Disciple

DISCIPLE FOR CHRIST
NKJV
1 TIMOTHY 4:12

Let no one despise your youth, but be an
example to the believers in word, in conduct,
in love, in spirit, in faith, in purity.

1 TIMOTHY 4:12

Growing Disciple

DISCIPLE FOR CHRIST
NKJV
COLOSSIANS 4:5

Walk in wisdom toward those who are outside,
redeeming the time.

COLOSSIANS 4:5

Growing Disciple

LOVE
NKJV
PSALM 89:1-2

I will sing of the mercies of the LORD forever;
With my mouth will I make known Your faith-
    fulness to all generations.
For I have said,
    "Mercy shall be built up forever;
Your faithfulness You shall establish in the
    very heavens."

PSALM 89:1-2

Life Issues

LOVE
NKJV
JAMES 1:19-20

Therefore, my beloved brethren, let every man
be swift to hear, slow to speak, slow to wrath;
for the wrath of man does not produce the
righteousness of God.

JAMES 1:19-20

Life Issues

LOVE
NKJV
JOHN 15:17

"These things I command you, that you love
one another."

JOHN 15:17

Life Issues

LOVE
NKJV
1 JOHN 4:11

Beloved, if God so loved us, we also ought to
love one another.

1 JOHN 4:11

Life Issues

PRAYER
PSALM 62:8

NIV

Trust in him at all times, O people;
    pour out your hearts to him,
    for God is our refuge.

PSALM 62:8

Life Issues

PRAYER
1 SAMUEL 12:23

NIV

As for me, far be it from me that I should sin against the LORD by failing to pray for you. And I will teach you the way that is good and right.

1 SAMUEL 12:23

Life Issues

PRAYER
1 THESSALONIANS 5:17-18

NIV

Pray continually; give thanks in all circumstances, for this is God's will for you in Christ Jesus.

1 THESSALONIANS 5:17-18

Life Issues

PRAYER
MATTHEW 6:9-13

NIV

"This . . . is how you should pray:
'Our Father in heaven,
hallowed be your name,
your kingdom come,
your will be done on earth as it is in heaven.
Give us today our daily bread.
Forgive us our debts, as we also have forgiven our
    debtors.
And lead us not into temptation,
but deliver us from the evil one.'"

MATTHEW 6:9-13

Life Issues

PURITY
PSALM 51:10

NIV

Create in me a pure heart, O God,
    and renew a steadfast spirit within me.

PSALM 51:10

Life Issues

PURITY
PHILIPPIANS 4:8

NIV

Brothers, whatever is true, whatever is noble, whatever is right, whatever is pure, whatever is lovely, whatever is admirable—if anything is excellent or praiseworthy—think about such things.

PHILIPPIANS 4:8

Life Issues

PURITY
ROMANS 6:13

NIV

Do not offer the parts of your body to sin, as instruments of wickedness, but rather offer yourselves to God, as those who have been brought from death to life; and offer the parts of your body to him as instruments of righteousness.

ROMANS 6:13

Life Issues

PURITY
PROVERBS 4:23

NIV

Above all else, guard your heart,
    for it is the wellspring of life.

PROVERBS 4:23

Life Issues

Life Issues

PRAYER NLT
1 Samuel 12:23

As for me, I will certainly not sin against the Lord by ending my prayers for you. And I will continue to teach you what is good and right.

1 Samuel 12:23

Life Issues

PRAYER Matthew 6:9-13   NLT
"Pray like this:
   Our Father in heaven,
      may your name be honored.
   May your Kingdom come soon.
   May your will be done here on earth,
      just as it is in heaven.
   Give us our food for today,
   and forgive us our sins,
      just as we have forgiven those who have
         sinned against us.
   And don't let us yield to temptation,
      but deliver us from the evil one."

Life Issues Matthew 6:9-13

PURITY NLT
Philippians 4:8

And now, dear brothers and sisters, let me say one more thing as I close this letter. Fix your thoughts on what is true and honorable and right. Think about things that are pure and lovely and admirable. Think about things that are excellent and worthy of praise.

Philippians 4:8

Life Issues

PURITY NLT
Proverbs 4:23

Above all else, guard your heart, for it affects everything you do.

Proverbs 4:23

Life Issues

PRAYER NLT
Psalm 62:8

O my people, trust in him at all times.
   Pour out your heart to him,
   for God is our refuge.

Psalm 62:8

Life Issues

PRAYER NLT
1 Thessalonians 5:17-18

Keep on praying. No matter what happens, always be thankful, for this is God's will for you who belong to Christ Jesus.

1 Thessalonians 5:17-18

Life Issues

PURITY NLT
Psalm 51:10

Create in me a clean heart, O God.
   Renew a right spirit within me.

Psalm 51:10

Life Issues

PURITY NLT
Romans 6:13

Do not let any part of your body become a tool of wickedness, to be used for sinning. Instead, give yourselves completely to God since you have been given new life. And use your whole body as a tool to do what is right for the glory of God.

Romans 6:13

Life Issues

LIFE ISSUES

PRAYER KJV
PSALM 62:8

Trust in him at all times; ye people, pour out your heart before him: God is a refuge for us. Selah.

PSALM 62:8

PRAYER KJV
1 SAMUEL 12:23

Moreover as for me, God forbid that I should sin against the LORD in ceasing to pray for you: but I will teach you the good and the right way.

1 SAMUEL 12:23

PRAYER KJV
1 THESSALONIANS 5:17-18

Pray without ceasing.
    In every thing give thanks: for this is the will of God in Christ Jesus concerning you.

1 THESSALONIANS 5:17-18

PRAYER   MATTHEW 6:9-13   KJV

After this manner therefore pray ye: Our Father which art in heaven, Hallowed be thy name.
    Thy kingdom come. Thy will be done in earth, as it is in heaven.
    Give us this day our daily bread.
    And forgive us our debts, as we forgive our debtors.
    And lead us not into temptation, but deliver us from evil: For thine is the kingdom, and the power, and the glory, for ever. Amen.

MATTHEW 6:9-13

PURITY KJV
PSALM 51:10

Create in me a clean heart, O God; and renew a right spirit within me.

PSALM 51:10

PURITY KJV
PHILIPPIANS 4:8

Finally, brethren, whatsoever things are true, whatsoever things are honest, whatsoever things are just, whatsoever things are pure, whatsoever things are lovely, whatsoever things are of good report; if there be any virtue, and if there be any praise, think on these things.

PHILIPPIANS 4:8

PURITY KJV
ROMANS 6:13

Neither yield ye your members as instruments of unrighteousness unto sin: but yield yourselves unto God, as those that are alive from the dead, and your members as instruments of righteousness unto God.

ROMANS 6:13

PURITY KJV
PROVERBS 4:23

Keep thy heart with all diligence; for out of it are the issues of life.

PROVERBS 4:23

PRAYER
NKJV
1 Samuel 12:23

Moreover, as for me, far be it from me that I should sin against the Lord in ceasing to pray for you; but I will teach you the good and the right way.

1 Samuel 12:23

Life Issues

PRAYER
NKJV
Psalm 62:8

Trust in Him at all times, you people;
Pour out your heart before Him;
God is a refuge for us. Selah

Psalm 62:8

Life Issues

PRAYER
Matthew 6:9-13
NKJV

"In this manner, therefore, pray:
Our Father in heaven,
Hallowed be Your name.
Your kingdom come.
Your will be done
On earth as it is in heaven.
Give us this day our daily bread.
And forgive us our debts,
As we forgive our debtors.
And do not lead us into temptation,
But deliver us from the evil one.
For Yours is the kingdom and the power and the
glory forever. Amen."

Life Issues

Matthew 6:9-13

PRAYER
NKJV
1 Thessalonians 5:17-18

Pray without ceasing, in everything give thanks; for this is the will of God in Christ Jesus for you.

1 Thessalonians 5:17-18

Life Issues

PURITY
NKJV
Philippians 4:8

Finally, brethren, whatever things are true, whatever things are noble, whatever things are just, whatever things are pure, whatever things are lovely, whatever things are of good report, if there is any virtue and if there is anything praiseworthy—meditate on these things.

Philippians 4:8

Life Issues

PURITY
NKJV
Psalm 51:10

Create in me a clean heart, O God,
And renew a steadfast spirit within me.

Psalm 51:10

Life Issues

PURITY
NKJV
Proverbs 4:23

Keep your heart with all diligence,
For out of it spring the issues of life.

Proverbs 4:23

Life Issues

PURITY
NKJV
Romans 6:13

And do not present your members as instruments of unrighteousness to sin, but present yourselves to God as being alive from the dead, and your members as instruments of righteousness to God.

Romans 6:13

Life Issues

Life Issues

GIVING NIV
Acts 4:32

All the believers were one in heart and mind. No one claimed that any of his possessions was his own, but they shared everything they had.

Acts 4:32

Life Issues

GIVING NIV
James 2:15-16

Suppose a brother or sister is without clothes and daily food. If one of you says to him, "Go, I wish you well; keep warm and well fed," but does nothing about his physical needs, what good is it?

James 2:15-16

Life Issues

GIVING NIV
1 Peter 4:10

Each one should use whatever gift he has received to serve others, faithfully administering God's grace in its various forms.

1 Peter 4:10

Life Issues

GIVING NIV
Luke 12:15

"Watch out! Be on your guard against all kinds of greed; a man's life does not consist in the abundance of his possessions."

Luke 12:15

Life Issues

HUMILITY NIV
1 Peter 3:8

All of you, live in harmony with one another; be sympathetic, love as brothers, be compassionate and humble.

1 Peter 3:8

Life Issues

HUMILITY NIV
Jeremiah 9:23

This is what the Lord says:

"Let not the wise man boast of his wisdom
    or the strong man boast of his strength
    or the rich man boast of his riches."

Jeremiah 9:23

Life Issues

HUMILITY NIV
Ephesians 4:2

Be completely humble and gentle; be patient, bearing with one another in love.

Ephesians 4:2

Life Issues

HUMILITY NIV
James 3:13

Who is wise and understanding among you? Let him show it by his good life, by deeds done in the humility that comes from wisdom.

James 3:1

Life Issues

LIFE ISSUES

GIVING NLT
JAMES 2:15-16

Suppose you see a brother or sister who needs food or clothing, and you say, "Well, good-bye and God bless you; stay warm and eat well"— but then you don't give that person any food or clothing. What good does that do?

JAMES 2:15-16

Life Issues

GIVING NLT
LUKE 12:15

Then he said, "Beware! Don't be greedy for what you don't have. Real life is not measured by how much we own."

LUKE 12:15

Life Issues

HUMILITY NLT
JEREMIAH 9:23

This is what the LORD says: "Let not the wise man gloat in his wisdom, or the mighty man in his might, or the rich man in his riches."

JEREMIAH 9:23

Life Issues

HUMILITY NLT
JAMES 3:13

If you are wise and understand God's ways, live a life of steady goodness so that only good deeds will pour forth. And if you don't brag about the good you do, then you will be truly wise!

JAMES 3:13

Life Issues

GIVING NLT
ACTS 4:32

All the believers were of one heart and mind, and they felt that what they owned was not their own; they shared everything they had.

ACTS 4:32

Life Issues

GIVING NLT
1 PETER 4:10

God has given gifts to each of you from his great variety of spiritual gifts. Manage them well so that God's generosity can flow through you.

1 PETER 4:10

Life Issues

HUMILITY NLT
1 PETER 3:8

Finally, all of you should be of one mind, full of sympathy toward each other, loving one another with tender hearts and humble minds.

1 PETER 3:8

Life Issues

HUMILITY NLT
EPHESIANS 4:2

Be humble and gentle. Be patient with each other, making allowance for each other's faults because of your love.

EPHESIANS 4:2

Life Issues

LIFE ISSUES

GIVING KJV
ACTS 4:32

And the multitude of them that believed were of one heart and of one soul: neither said any of them that aught of the things which he possessed was his own; but they had all things common.

ACTS 4:32

Life Issues

GIVING KJV
JAMES 2:15-16

If a brother or sister be naked, and destitute of daily food,
And one of you say unto them, Depart in peace, be ye warmed and filled; notwithstanding ye give them not those things which are needful to the body; what doth it profit?

JAMES 2:15-16

Life Issues

GIVING KJV
1 PETER 4:10

As every man hath received the gift, even so minister the same one to another, as good stewards of the manifold grace of God.

1 PETER 4:10

Life Issues

GIVING KJV

LUKE 12:15
And he said unto them, Take heed, and beware of covetousness: for a man's life consisteth not in the abundance of the things which he possesseth.

LUKE 12:15

Life Issues

HUMILITY KJV
1 PETER 3:8

Finally, be ye all of one mind, having compassion one of another, love as brethren, be pitiful, be courteous.

1 PETER 3:8

Life Issues

HUMILITY KJV
JEREMIAH 9:23

Thus saith the LORD, Let not the wise man glory in his wisdom, neither let the mighty man glory in his might, let not the rich man glory in his riches.

JEREMIAH 9:23

Life Issues

HUMILITY KJV
EPHESIANS 4:2

With all lowliness and meekness, with longsuffering, forbearing one another in love.

EPHESIANS 4:2

Life Issues

HUMILITY KJV
JAMES 3:13

Who is a wise man and endued with knowledge among you? let him shew out of a good conversation his works with meekness of wisdom.

JAMES 3:13

Life Issues

GIVING
NKJV
JAMES 2:15-16

If a brother or sister is naked and destitute of daily food, and one of you says to them, "Depart in peace, be warmed and filled," but you do not give them the things which are needed for the body, what does it profit?

JAMES 2:15-16

Life Issues

GIVING
NKJV
LUKE 12:15

And He said to them, "Take heed and beware of covetousness, for one's life does not consist in the abundance of the things he possesses."

LUKE 12:15

Life Issues

HUMILITY
NKJV
JEREMIAH 9:23

Thus says the LORD:

"Let not the wise man glory in his wisdom, Let not the mighty man glory in his might, Nor let the rich man glory in his riches."

JEREMIAH 9:23

Life Issues

HUMILITY
NKJV
JAMES 3:13

Who is wise and understanding among you? Let him show by good conduct that his works are done in the meekness of wisdom.

JAMES 3:13

Life Issues

GIVING
NKJV
ACTS 4:32

Now the multitude of those who believed were of one heart and one soul; neither did anyone say that any of the things he possessed was his own, but they had all things in common.

ACTS 4:32

Life Issues

GIVING
NKJV
1 PETER 4:10

As each one has received a gift, minister it to one another, as good stewards of the manifold grace of God.

1 PETER 4:10

Life Issues

HUMILITY
NKJV
1 PETER 3:8

Finally, all of you be of one mind, having compassion for one another; love as brothers, be tenderhearted, be courteous.

1 PETER 3:8

Life Issues

HUMILITY
NKJV
EPHESIANS 4:2

With all lowliness and gentleness, with long-suffering, bearing with one another in love.

EPHESIANS 4:2

Life Issues

Life Issues

PERSEVERANCE
NIV
JAMES 1:12

Blessed is the man who perseveres under trial, because when he has stood the test, he will receive the crown of life that God has promised to those who love him.

JAMES 1:12

Life Issues

PERSEVERANCE
NIV
2 TIMOTHY 2:3

Endure hardship with us like a good soldier of Christ Jesus.

2 TIMOTHY 2:3

Life Issues

PERSEVERANCE
NIV
HEBREWS 6:11-12

We want each of you to show this same diligence to the very end, in order to make your hope sure. We do not want you to become lazy, but to imitate those who through faith and patience inherit what has been promised.

HEBREWS 6:11-12

Life Issues

PERSEVERANCE
NIV
1 CORINTHIANS 4:2

It is required that those who have been given a trust must prove faithful.

1 CORINTHIANS 4:2

Life Issues

STUDY
NIV
1 CORINTHIANS 14:20

Brothers, stop thinking like children. In regard to evil be infants, but in your thinking be adults.

1 CORINTHIANS 14:20

Life Issues

STUDY
NIV
PSALM 119:34

Give me understanding, and I will keep your law and obey it with all my heart.

PSALM 119:34

Life Issues

STUDY
NIV
PROVERBS 9:10

The fear of the LORD is the beginning of wisdom, and knowledge of the Holy One is understanding.

PROVERBS 9:10

Life Issues

STUDY
NIV
DEUTERONOMY 4:9

Only be careful, and watch yourselves closely so that you do not forget the things your eyes have seen or let them slip from your heart as long as you live. Teach them to your children and to their children after them.

DEUTERONOMY 4:9

Life Issues

Life Issues

PERSEVERANCE ^{NLT}
2 Timothy 2:3

Endure suffering along with me, as a good soldier of Christ Jesus.

2 Timothy 2:3

Life Issues

PERSEVERANCE ^{NLT}
1 Corinthians 4:2

Now, a person who is put in charge as a manager must be faithful.

1 Corinthians 4:2

Life Issues

STUDY ^{NLT}
Psalm 119:34

Give me understanding and I will obey your
 law;
 I will put it into practice with all my heart.

Psalm 119:34

Life Issues

STUDY ^{NLT}
Deuteronomy 4:9

But watch out! Be very careful never to forget what you have seen the Lord do for you. Do not let these things escape from your mind as long as you live! And be sure to pass them on to your children and grandchildren.

Deuteronomy 4:9

Life Issues

PERSEVERANCE ^{NLT}
James 1:12

God blesses the people who patiently endure testing. Afterward they will receive the crown of life that God has promised to those who love him.

James 1:12

Life Issues

PERSEVERANCE ^{NLT}
Hebrews 6:11-12

Our great desire is that you will keep right on loving others as long as life lasts, in order to make certain that what you hope for will come true. Then you will not become spiritually dull and indifferent. Instead, you will follow the example of those who are going to inherit God's promises because of their faith and patience.

Hebrews 6:11-12

Life Issues

STUDY ^{NLT}
1 Corinthians 14:20

Dear brothers and sisters, don't be childish in your understanding of these things. Be innocent as babies when it comes to evil, but be mature and wise in understanding matters of this kind.

1 Corinthians 14:20

Life Issues

STUDY ^{NLT}
Proverbs 9:10

Fear of the Lord is the beginning of wisdom. Knowledge of the Holy One results in understanding.

Proverbs 9:10

Life Issues

PERSEVERANCE KJV
JAMES 1:12

Blessed is the man that endureth temptation: for when he is tried, he shall receive the crown of life, which the Lord hath promised to them that love him.

JAMES 1:12

Life Issues

PERSEVERANCE KJV
2 TIMOTHY 2:3

Thou therefore endure hardness, as a good soldier of Jesus Christ.

2 TIMOTHY 2:3

Life Issues

PERSEVERANCE KJV
HEBREWS 6:11-12

And we desire that every one of you do shew the same diligence to the full assurance of hope unto the end:
  That ye be not slothful, but followers of them who through faith and patience inherit the promises.

HEBREWS 6:11-12

Life Issues

PERSEVERANCE KJV
1 CORINTHIANS 4:2

Moreover it is required in stewards, that a man be found faithful.

1 CORINTHIANS 4:2

Life Issues

STUDY KJV
1 CORINTHIANS 14:20

Brethren, be not children in understanding: howbeit in malice be ye children, but in understanding be men.

1 CORINTHIANS 14:20

Life Issues

STUDY KJV
PSALM 119:34

Give me understanding, and I shall keep thy law; yea, I shall observe it with my whole heart.

PSALM 119:34

Life Issues

STUDY KJV
PROVERBS 9:10

The fear of the LORD is the beginning of wisdom: and the knowledge of the holy is understanding.

PROVERBS 9:10

Life Issues

STUDY KJV
DEUTERONOMY 4:9

Only take heed to thyself, and keep thy soul diligently, lest thou forget the things which thine eyes have seen, and lest they depart from thy heart all the days of thy life: but teach them thy sons, and thy sons' sons.

DEUTERONOMY 4:9

Life Issues

Life Issues

PERSEVERANCE NKJV
2 Timothy 2:3

You therefore must endure hardship as a good soldier of Jesus Christ.

2 Timothy 2:3

Life Issues

PERSEVERANCE NKJV
James 1:12

Blessed is the man who endures temptation; for when he has been approved, he will receive the crown of life which the Lord has promised to those who love Him.

James 1:12

Life Issues

PERSEVERANCE NKJV
1 Corinthians 4:2

Moreover it is required in stewards that one be found faithful.

1 Corinthians 4:2

Life Issues

PERSEVERANCE NKJV
Hebrews 6:11-12

And we desire that each one of you show the same diligence to the full assurance of hope until the end, that you do not become sluggish, but imitate those who through faith and patience inherit the promises.

Hebrews 6:11-12

Life Issues

STUDY NKJV
Psalm 119:34

Give me understanding,
	and I shall keep Your law;
Indeed, I shall observe it with my
	whole heart.

Psalm 119:34

Life Issues

STUDY NKJV
1 Corinthians 14:20

Brethren, do not be children in understanding; however, in malice be babes, but in understanding be mature.

1 Corinthians 14:20

Life Issues

STUDY NKJV
Deuteronomy 4:9

Only take heed to yourself, and diligently keep yourself, lest you forget the things your eyes have seen, and lest they depart from your heart all the days of your life. And teach them to your children and your grandchildren.

Deuteronomy 4:9

Life Issues

STUDY NKJV
Proverbs 9:10

The fear of the Lord
	is the beginning of wisdom,
And the knowledge of the Holy One
	is understanding.

Proverbs 9:10

Life Issues

WORSHIP   NIV
PSALM 95:6-7

Come, let us bow down in worship,
    let us kneel before the LORD our Maker;
for he is our God
    and we are the people of his pasture,
    the flock under his care.

PSALM 95:6-7

Life Issues

WORSHIP   NIV
JOHN 4:24

"God is spirit, and his worshipers must worship
in spirit and in truth."

JOHN 4:24

Life Issues

WORSHIP   NIV
HEBREWS 13:15

Through Jesus . . . let us continually offer to
God a sacrifice of praise—the fruit of lips that
confess his name.

HEBREWS 13:15

Life Issues

WORSHIP   NIV
EPHESIANS 1:5-6

He predestined us to be adopted as his sons
through Jesus Christ, in accordance with his
pleasure and will—to the praise of his glorious
grace, which he has freely given us in the One
he loves.

EPHESIANS 1:5-6

Life Issues

WITNESS BY LOVE   NIV
1 THESSALONIANS 3:12

May the Lord make your love increase and
overflow for each other and for everyone else,
just as ours does for you.

1 THESSALONIANS 3:12

Leadership

WITNESS BY LOVE   NIV
JOHN 15:12

"My command is this: Love each other as I
have loved you."

JOHN 15:12

Leadership

WITNESS BY LOVE   NIV
LUKE 6:27-28

"I tell you who hear me: Love your enemies,
do good to those who hate you, bless those
who curse you, pray for those who mistreat
you."

LUKE 6:27-28

Leadership

WITNESS BY LOVE   NIV
1 CORINTHIANS 13:4-5

Love is patient, love is kind. It does not envy, it
does not boast, it is not proud. It is not rude,
it is not self-seeking, it is not easily angered, it
keeps no record of wrongs.

1 CORINTHIANS 13:4-5

Leadership

WORSHIP
JOHN 4:24

NLT

"For God is Spirit, so those who worship him must worship in spirit and in truth."

JOHN 4:24

Life Issues

WORSHIP
EPHESIANS 1:5-6

NLT

His unchanging plan has always been to adopt us into his own family by bringing us to himself through Jesus Christ. And this gave him great pleasure.

So we praise God for the wonderful kindness he has poured out on us because we belong to his dearly loved Son.

EPHESIANS 1:5-6

Life Issues

WITNESS BY LOVE
JOHN 15:12

NLT

"I command you to love each other in the same way that I love you."

JOHN 15:12

Leadership

WITNESS BY LOVE
1 CORINTHIANS 13:4-5

NLT

Love is patient and kind. Love is not jealous or boastful or proud or rude. Love does not demand its own way. Love is not irritable, and it keeps no record of when it has been wronged.

1 CORINTHIANS 13:4-5

Leadership

WORSHIP
PSALM 95:6-7

NLT

Come, let us worship and bow down.
Let us kneel before the LORD our maker,
for he is our God.
We are the people he watches over,
the sheep under his care.

PSALM 95:6-7

Life Issues

WORSHIP
HEBREWS 13:15

NLT

With Jesus' help, let us continually offer our sacrifice of praise to God by proclaiming the glory of his name.

HEBREWS 13:15

Life Issues

WITNESS BY LOVE
1 THESSALONIANS 3:12

NLT

And may the Lord make your love grow and overflow to each other and to everyone else, just as our love overflows toward you.

1 THESSALONIANS 3:12

Leadership

WITNESS BY LOVE
LUKE 6:27-28

NLT

"But if you are willing to listen, I say, love your enemies. Do good to those who hate you. Pray for the happiness of those who curse you. Pray for those who hurt you."

LUKE 6:27-28

Leadership

WORSHIP KJV
PSALM 95:6-7

O come, let us worship and bow down: let us kneel before the LORD our maker.
  For he is our God; and we are the people of his pasture, and the sheep of his hand.

PSALM 95:6-7

Life Issues

WORSHIP KJV
JOHN 4:24

God is a Spirit: and they that worship him must worship him in spirit and in truth.

JOHN 4:24

Life Issues

WORSHIP KJV
HEBREWS 13:15

By him therefore let us offer the sacrifice of praise to God continually, that is, the fruit of our lips giving thanks to his name.

HEBREWS 13:15

Life Issues

WORSHIP KJV
EPHESIANS 1:5-6

Having predestinated us unto the adoption of children by Jesus Christ to himself, according to the good pleasure of his will,
  To the praise of the glory of his grace, wherein he hath made us accepted in the beloved.

EPHESIANS 1:5-6

Life Issues

WITNESS BY LOVE KJV
1 THESSALONIANS 3:12

And the Lord make you to increase and abound in love one toward another, and toward all men, even as we do toward you.

1 THESSALONIANS 3:12

Leadership

WITNESS BY LOVE KJV
JOHN 15:12

This is my commandment, That ye love one another, as I have loved you.

JOHN 15:12

Leadership

WITNESS BY LOVE KJV
LUKE 6:27-28

But I say unto you which hear, Love your enemies, do good to them which hate you,
  Bless them that curse you, and pray for them which despitefully use you.

LUKE 6:27-28

Leadership

WITNESS BY LOVE KJV
1 CORINTHIANS 13:4-5

Charity suffereth long, and is kind; charity envieth not; charity vaunteth not itself, is not puffed up,
  Doth not behave itself unseemly, seeketh not her own, is not easily provoked, thinketh no evil.

1 CORINTHIANS 13:4-5

Leadership

WORSHIP
NKJV
JOHN 4:24

"God is Spirit, and those who worship Him must worship in spirit and truth."

JOHN 4:24

Life Issues

WORSHIP
NKJV
EPHESIANS 1:5-6

Having predestined us to adoption as sons by Jesus Christ to Himself, according to the good pleasure of His will, to the praise of the glory of His grace, by which He made us accepted in the Beloved.

EPHESIANS 1:5-6

Life Issues

WITNESS BY LOVE
NKJV
JOHN 15:12

"This is My commandment, that you love one another as I have loved you."

JOHN 15:12

Leadership

WITNESS BY LOVE
NKJV
1 CORINTHIANS 13:4-5

Love suffers long and is kind; love does not envy; love does not parade itself, is not puffed up; does not behave rudely, does not seek its own, is not provoked, thinks no evil.

1 CORINTHIANS 13:4-5

Leadership

WORSHIP
NKJV
PSALM 95:6-7

Oh come, let us worship
and bow down;
Let us kneel before the LORD our
Maker.
For He is our God,
And we are the people of His pasture,
And the sheep of His hand.

PSALM 95:6-7

Life Issues

WORSHIP
NKJV
HEBREWS 13:15

Therefore by Him let us continually offer the sacrifice of praise to God, that is, the fruit of our lips, giving thanks to His name.

HEBREWS 13:15

Life Issues

WITNESS BY LOVE
NKJV
1 THESSALONIANS 3:12

And may the Lord make you increase and abound in love to one another and to all, just as we do to you.

1 THESSALONIANS 3:12

Leadership

WITNESS BY LOVE
NKJV
LUKE 6:27-28

"But I say to you who hear: Love your enemies, do good to those who hate you, bless those who curse you, and pray for those who spitefully use you."

LUKE 6:27-28

Leadership

WITNESS BY LOVE
NIV

1 PETER 4:8

Above all, love each other deeply, because love covers over a multitude of sins.

1 PETER 4:8

WITNESS BY LOVE
NIV

MATTHEW 5:44

"I tell you: Love your enemies and pray for those who persecute you."

MATTHEW 5:44

WITNESS BY LIFE
NIV

LUKE 22:26

"You are not to be like that. Instead, the greatest among you should be like the youngest, and the one who rules like the one who serves."

LUKE 22:26

WITNESS BY LIFE
NIV

EPHESIANS 5:17

Do not be foolish, but understand what the Lord's will is.

EPHESIANS 5:17

WITNESS BY LIFE
NIV

1 CORINTHIANS 8:9

Be careful . . . that the exercise of your freedom does not become a stumbling block to the weak.

1 CORINTHIANS 8:9

WITNESS BY LIFE
NIV

2 TIMOTHY 2:2

The things you have heard me say in the presence of many witnesses entrust to reliable men who will also be qualified to teach others.

2 TIMOTHY 2:2

WITNESS BY LIFE
NIV

1 PETER 1:15-16

Just as he who called you is holy, so be holy in all you do; for it is written: "Be holy, because I am holy."

1 PETER 1:15-16

WITNESS BY LIFE
NIV

GALATIANS 5:22-23

The fruit of the Spirit is love, joy, peace, patience, kindness, goodness, faithfulness, gentleness and self-control. Against such things there is no law.

GALATIANS 5:22-23

WITNESS BY LOVE NLT
MATTHEW 5:44

"But I say, love your enemies! Pray for those who persecute you!"

MATTHEW 5:44

Leadership

WITNESS BY LIFE NLT
EPHESIANS 5:17

Don't act thoughtlessly, but try to understand what the Lord wants you to do.

EPHESIANS 5:17

Leadership

WITNESS BY LIFE NLT
2 TIMOTHY 2:2

You have heard me teach many things that have been confirmed by many reliable witnesses. Teach these great truths to trustworthy people who are able to pass them on to others.

2 TIMOTHY 2:2

Leadership

WITNESS BY LIFE NLT
GALATIANS 5:22-23

But when the Holy Spirit controls our lives, he will produce this kind of fruit in us: love, joy, peace, patience, kindness, goodness, faithfulness, gentleness, and self-control. Here there is no conflict with the law.

GALATIANS 5:22-23

Leadership

WITNESS BY LOVE NLT
1 PETER 4:8

Most important of all, continue to show deep love for each other, for love covers a multitude of sins.

1 PETER 4:8

Leadership

WITNESS BY LIFE NLT
LUKE 22:26

"But among you, those who are the greatest should take the lowest rank, and the leader should be like a servant."

LUKE 22:26

Leadership

WITNESS BY LIFE NLT
1 CORINTHIANS 8:9

But you must be careful with this freedom of yours. Do not cause a brother or sister with a weaker conscience to stumble.

1 CORINTHIANS 8:9

Leadership

WITNESS BY LIFE NLT
1 PETER 1:15-16

But now you must be holy in everything you do, just as God—who chose you to be his children—is holy. For he himself has said, "You must be holy because I am holy."

1 PETER 1:15-16

Leadership

LEADERSHIP

WITNESS BY LOVE   KJV
1 PETER 4:8

And above all things have fervent charity among yourselves: for charity shall cover the multitude of sins.

          1 PETER 4:8

Leadership

WITNESS BY LOVE   KJV
MATTHEW 5:44

But I say unto you, Love your enemies, bless them that curse you, do good to them that hate you, and pray for them which despitefully use you, and persecute you.

          MATTHEW 5:44

Leadership

WITNESS BY LIFE   KJV
LUKE 22:26

But ye shall not be so: but he that is greatest among you, let him be as the younger; and he that is chief, as he that doth serve.

          LUKE 22:26

Leadership

WITNESS BY LIFE   KJV
EPHESIANS 5:17

Wherefore be ye not unwise, but understanding what the will of the Lord is.

          EPHESIANS 5:17

Leadership

WITNESS BY LIFE   KJV
1 CORINTHIANS 8:9

But take heed lest by any means this liberty of yours become a stumblingblock to them that are weak.

          1 CORINTHIANS 8:9

Leadership

WITNESS BY LIFE   KJV
2 TIMOTHY 2:2

And the things that thou hast heard of me among many witnesses, the same commit thou to faithful men, who shall be able to teach others also.

          2 TIMOTHY 2:2

Leadership

WITNESS BY LIFE   KJV
1 PETER 1:15-16

But as he which hath called you is holy, so be ye holy in all manner of conversation;
    Because it is written, Be ye holy; for I am holy.

          1 PETER 1:15-16

Leadership

WITNESS BY LIFE   KJV
GALATIANS 5:22-23

But the fruit of the Spirit is love, joy, peace, longsuffering, gentleness, goodness, faith,
    Meekness, temperance: against such there is no law.

          GALATIANS 5:22-23

Leadership

LEADERSHIP

WITNESS BY LOVE NKJV
MATTHEW 5:44

"But I say to you, love your enemies, bless those who curse you, do good to those who hate you, and pray for those who spitefully use you and persecute you."

MATTHEW 5:44

Leadership

WITNESS BY LIFE NKJV
EPHESIANS 5:17

Therefore do not be unwise, but understand what the will of the Lord is.

EPHESIANS 5:17

Leadership

WITNESS BY LIFE NKJV
2 TIMOTHY 2:2

And the things that you have heard from me among many witnesses, commit these to faithful men who will be able to teach others also.

2 TIMOTHY 2:2

Leadership

WITNESS BY LIFE NKJV
GALATIANS 5:22-23

But the fruit of the Spirit is love, joy, peace, longsuffering, kindness, goodness, faithfulness, gentleness, self-control. Against such there is no law.

GALATIANS 5:22-23

Leadership

WITNESS BY LOVE NKJV
1 PETER 4:8

And above all things have fervent love for one another, for "love will cover a multitude of sins."

1 PETER 4:8

Leadership

WITNESS BY LIFE NKJV
LUKE 22:26

"But not so among you; on the contrary, he who is greatest among you, let him be as the younger, and he who governs as he who serves."

LUKE 22:26

Leadership

WITNESS BY LIFE NKJV
1 CORINTHIANS 8:9

But beware lest somehow this liberty of yours become a stumbling block to those who are weak.

1 CORINTHIANS 8:9

Leadership

WITNESS BY LIFE NKJV
1 PETER 1:15-16

But as He who called you is holy, you also be holy in all your conduct, because it is written, "Be holy, for I am holy."

1 PETER 1:15-16

Leadership

WITNESS BY JUSTICE NIV
DEUTERONOMY 27:19

Cursed is the man who withholds justice from
the alien, the fatherless or the widow.
Then all the people shall say,
"Amen!"

DEUTERONOMY 27:19

Leadership

WITNESS BY JUSTICE NIV
PSALM 106:3

Blessed are they who maintain justice,
who constantly do what is right.

PSALM 106:3

Leadership

WITNESS BY JUSTICE NIV
PROVERBS 21:3

To do what is right and just
is more acceptable to the LORD than sacrifice.

PROVERBS 21:3

Leadership

WITNESS BY JUSTICE NIV
ISAIAH 1:17

"Learn to do right!
Seek justice,
encourage the oppressed.
Defend the cause of the fatherless,
plead the case of the widow."

ISAIAH 1:17

Leadership

WITNESS BY JUSTICE NIV
JEREMIAH 9:24

"Let him who boasts boast about this:
that he understands and knows me,
that I am the LORD, who exercises kindness,
justice and righteousness on earth,
for in these I delight,"
declares the LORD.

JEREMIAH 9:24

Leadership

WITNESS BY JUSTICE NIV
ZECHARIAH 7:9

"This is what the LORD Almighty says:
'Administer true justice; show mercy and compassion to one another.'"

ZECHARIAH 7:9

Leadership

WITNESS BY WORD NIV
MARK 16:15

He said to them, "Go into all the world and
preach the good news to all creation."

MARK 16:15

Leadership

WITNESS BY WORD NIV
LUKE 6:45

"The good man brings good things out of the
good stored up in his heart, and the evil man
brings evil things out of the evil stored up in
his heart. For out of the overflow of his heart
his mouth speaks."

LUKE 6:45

Leadership

Leadership

WITNESS BY JUSTICE
PSALM 106:3

NLT

Happy are those who deal justly with others
and always do what is right.

PSALM 106:3

WITNESS BY JUSTICE
DEUTERONOMY 27:19

NLT

Cursed is anyone who is unjust to foreigners,
orphans, and widows.
And all the people will reply, "Amen."

DEUTERONOMY 27:19

WITNESS BY JUSTICE
ISAIAH 1:17

NLT

"Learn to do good. Seek justice. Help the
oppressed. Defend the orphan. Fight for the
rights of widows."

ISAIAH 1:17

WITNESS BY JUSTICE
PROVERBS 21:3

NLT

The LORD is more pleased when we do what
is just and right than when we give him
sacrifices.

PROVERBS 21:3

WITNESS BY JUSTICE
ZECHARIAH 7:9

NLT

"This is what the LORD Almighty says: Judge
fairly and honestly, and show mercy and
kindness to one another."

ZECHARIAH 7:9

WITNESS BY JUSTICE
JEREMIAH 9:24

NLT

"Let them boast in this alone: that they truly
know me and understand that I am the LORD
who is just and righteous, whose love is
unfailing, and that I delight in these things. I,
the LORD, have spoken!"

JEREMIAH 9:24

WITNESS BY WORD
LUKE 6:45

NLT

"A good person produces good deeds from a
good heart, and an evil person produces evil
deeds from an evil heart. Whatever is in your
heart determines what you say."

LUKE 6:45

WITNESS BY WORD
MARK 16:15

NLT

And then he told them, "Go into all the world
and preach the Good News to everyone,
everywhere."

MARK 16:15

WITNESS BY JUSTICE
DEUTERONOMY 27:19

KJV

Cursed be he that perverteth the judgment of the stranger, fatherless, and widow. And all the people shall say, Amen.

DEUTERONOMY 27:19

Leadership

WITNESS BY JUSTICE
PSALM 106:3

KJV

Blessed are they that keep judgment, and he that doeth righteousness at all times.

PSALM 106:3

Leadership

WITNESS BY JUSTICE
PROVERBS 21:3

KJV

To do justice and judgment is more acceptable to the LORD than sacrifice.

PROVERBS 21:3

Leadership

WITNESS BY JUSTICE
ISAIAH 1:17

KJV

Learn to do well; seek judgment, relieve the oppressed, judge the fatherless, plead for the widow.

ISAIAH 1:17

Leadership

WITNESS BY JUSTICE
JEREMIAH 9:24

KJV

But let him that glorieth glory in this, that he understandeth and knoweth me, that I am the LORD which exercise lovingkindness, judgment, and righteousness, in the earth: for in these things I delight, saith the LORD.

JEREMIAH 9:24

Leadership

WITNESS BY JUSTICE
ZECHARIAH 7:9

KJV

Thus speaketh the LORD of hosts, saying, Execute true judgment, and shew mercy and compassions every man to his brother.

ZECHARIAH 7:9

Leadership

WITNESS BY WORD
MARK 16:15

KJV

And he said unto them, Go ye into all the world, and preach the gospel to every creature.

MARK 16:15

Leadership

WITNESS BY WORD
LUKE 6:45

KJV

A good man out of the good treasure of his heart bringeth forth that which is good; and an evil man out of the evil treasure of his heart bringeth forth that which is evil: for of the abundance of the heart his mouth speaketh.

LUKE 6:45

Leadership

LEADERSHIP

WITNESS BY JUSTICE
PSALM 106:3
NKJV

Blessed are those who keep justice,
  And he who does righteousness at all
    times!

PSALM 106:3

WITNESS BY JUSTICE
ISAIAH 1:17
NKJV

"Learn to do good;
  Seek justice,
  Rebuke the oppressor;
  Defend the fatherless,
  Plead for the widow."

ISAIAH 1:17

WITNESS BY JUSTICE
ZECHARIAH 7:9
NKJV

"Thus says the LORD of hosts:
  'Execute true justice,
  Show mercy and compassion
  Everyone to his brother.'"

ZECHARIAH 7:9

WITNESS BY WORD
LUKE 6:45
NKJV

"A good man out of the good treasure of his heart brings forth good; and an evil man out of the evil treasure of his heart brings forth evil. For out of the abundance of the heart his mouth speaks."

LUKE 6:45

WITNESS BY JUSTICE
DEUTERONOMY 27:19
NKJV

Cursed is the one who perverts the justice due the stranger, the fatherless, and widow. And all the people shall say, "Amen!"

DEUTERONOMY 27:19

WITNESS BY JUSTICE
PROVERBS 21:3
NKJV

To do righteousness and justice
  Is more acceptable to the LORD than
  ˙ sacrifice.

PROVERBS 21:3

WITNESS BY JUSTICE
JEREMIAH 9:24
NKJV

"But let him who glories glory in this,
  That he understands and knows Me,
  That I am the LORD, exercising lovingkind-
    ness, judgment, and righteousness in
    the earth.
  For in these I delight," says the LORD.

JEREMIAH 9:24

WITNESS BY WORD
MARK 16:15
NKJV

And He said to them, "Go into all the world and preach the gospel to every creature."

MARK 16:15

WITNESS BY WORD   NIV
1 CORINTHIANS 2:12-13

We have not received the spirit of the world but the Spirit who is from God, that we may understand what God has freely given us. This is what we speak, not in words taught us by human wisdom but in words taught by the Spirit, expressing spiritual truths in spiritual words.

1 CORINTHIANS 2:12-13

Leadership

WITNESS BY WORD   NIV
EPHESIANS 6:19

Pray also for me, that whenever I open my mouth, words may be given me so that I will fearlessly make known the mystery of the gospel.

EPHESIANS 6:19

Leadership

WITNESS BY WORD   NIV
PROVERBS 16:24

Pleasant words are a honeycomb,
    sweet to the soul and healing to the bones.

PROVERBS 16:24

Leadership

WITNESS BY WORD   NIV
2 TIMOTHY 2:15

Do your best to present yourself to God as one approved, a workman who does not need to be ashamed and who correctly handles the word of truth.

2 TIMOTHY 2:15

Leadership

LEADERSHIP

WITNESS BY WORD
<small>NLT</small>
EPHESIANS 6:19

And pray for me, too. Ask God to give me the right words as I boldly explain God's secret plan that the Good News is for the Gentiles, too.

EPHESIANS 6:19

Leadership

WITNESS BY WORD
<small>NLT</small>
2 TIMOTHY 2:15

Work hard so God can approve you. Be a good worker, one who does not need to be ashamed and who correctly explains the word of truth.

2 TIMOTHY 2:15

Leadership

WITNESS BY WORD
<small>NLT</small>
1 CORINTHIANS 2:12-13

And God has actually given us his Spirit (not the world's spirit) so we can know the wonderful things God has freely given us. When we tell you this, we do not use words of human wisdom. We speak words given to us by the Spirit, using the Spirit's words to explain spiritual truths.

1 CORINTHIANS 2:12-13

Leadership

WITNESS BY WORD
<small>NLT</small>
PROVERBS 16:24

Kind words are like honey—sweet to the soul and healthy for the body.

PROVERBS 16:24

Leadership

WITNESS BY WORD
1 CORINTHIANS 2:12-13 — KJV

Now we have received, not the spirit of the world, but the spirit which is of God; that we might know the things that are freely given to us of God.

Which things also we speak, not in the words which man's wisdom teacheth, but which the Holy Ghost teacheth; comparing spiritual things with spiritual.

1 CORINTHIANS 2:12-13

Leadership

WITNESS BY WORD
EPHESIANS 6:19 — KJV

And for me, that utterance may be given unto me, that I may open my mouth boldly, to make known the mystery of the gospel.

EPHESIANS 6:19

Leadership

WITNESS BY WORD
PROVERBS 16:24 — KJV

Pleasant words are as an honeycomb, sweet to the soul, and health to the bones.

PROVERBS 16:24

Leadership

WITNESS BY WORD
2 TIMOTHY 2:15 — KJV

Study to shew thyself approved unto God, a workman that needeth not to be ashamed, rightly dividing the word of truth.

2 TIMOTHY 2:15

Leadership

LEADERSHIP

WITNESS BY WORD
NKJV
EPHESIANS 6:19

And for me, that utterance may be given to me, that I may open my mouth boldly to make known the mystery of the gospel.

EPHESIANS 6:19

Leadership

WITNESS BY WORD
NKJV
1 CORINTHIANS 2:12-13

Now we have received, not the spirit of the world, but the Spirit who is from God, that we might know the things that have been freely given to us by God.

These things we also speak, not in words which man's wisdom teaches but which the Holy Spirit teaches, comparing spiritual things with spiritual.

1 CORINTHIANS 2:12-13

Leadership

WITNESS BY WORD
NKJV
2 TIMOTHY 2:15

Be diligent to present yourself approved to God, a worker who does not need to be ashamed, rightly dividing the word of truth.

2 TIMOTHY 2:15

Leadership

WITNESS BY WORD
NKJV
PROVERBS 16:24

Pleasant words are like a honeycomb,
Sweetness to the soul and health to the bones.

PROVERBS 16:24

Leadership